Aristophane's Apology by Robert Browning

INCLUDING A TRANSCRIPT FROM EURIPIDES, BEING THE LAST ADVENTURE OF BALAUSTION

Robert Browning is one of the most significant Victorian Poets and, of course, English Poetry.

Much of his reputation is based upon his mastery of the dramatic monologue although his talents encompassed verse plays and even a well-regarded essay on Shelley during a long and prolific career.

He was born on May 7th, 1812 in Walmouth, London. Much of his education was home based and Browning was an eclectic and studious student, learning several languages and much else across a myriad of subjects, interests and passions.

Browning's early career began promisingly. The fragment from his intended long poem Pauline brought him to the attention of Dante Gabriel Rossetti, and was followed by Paracelsus, which was praised by both William Wordsworth and Charles Dickens. In 1840 the difficult Sordello, which was seen as willfully obscure, brought his career almost to a standstill.

Despite these artistic and professional difficulties his personal life was about to become immensely fulfilling. He began a relationship with, and then married, the older and better known Elizabeth Barrett. This new foundation served to energise his writings, his life and his career.

During their time in Italy they both wrote much of their best work. With her untimely death in 1861 he returned to London and thereafter began several further major projects.

The collection Dramatis Personae (1864) and the book-length epic poem The Ring and the Book (1868-69) were published and well received; his reputation as a venerated English poet now assured.

Robert Browning died in Venice on December 12th, 1889.

Index of Contents

ARISTOPHANE'S APOLOGY
Robert Browning – A Short Biography
Robert Browning – A Concise Bibliography

οὐκ ἔσθω κενέβρει'· ὁπόταν δὲ θύῃς
τι, κάλει με.

"I eat no carrion; when you sacrifice
Some cleanly creature—call me for a slice!"

ARISTOPHANE'S APOLOGY

Wind, wave, and bark, bear Euthukles and me,
Balaustion, from—not sorrow but despair,
Not memory but the present and its pang!
Athenai, live thou hearted in my heart:
Never, while I live, may I see thee more,
Never again may these repugnant orbs
Ache themselves blind before the hideous pomp,
The ghastly mirth which mocked thine overthrow
—Death's entry, Haides' outrage!
                    Doomed to die,—
Fire should have flung a passion of embrace
About thee till, resplendently inarmed,
(Temple by temple folded to his breast,
All thy white wonder fainting out in ash,)
Lightly some vaporous sigh of soul escaped
And so the Immortals bade Athenai back!
Or earth might sunder and absorb thee, save,
Buried below Olumpos and its gods,
Akropolis to dominate her realm
For Koré, and console the ghosts; or, sea,
What if thy watery plural vastitude,
Rolling unanimous advance, had rushed,
Might upon might, a moment,—stood, one stare,
Sea-face to city-face, thy glaucous wave
Glassing that marbled last magnificence,—
Till fate's pale tremulous foam-flower tipped the gray,
And when wave broke and overswarmed, and, sucked
To bounds back, multitudinously ceased,
Let land again breathe unconfused with sea,
Attiké was, Athenai was not now!

Such end I could have borne, for I had shared.
But this which, glanced at, aches within my orbs
To blinding,—bear me thence, bark, wind and wave!
Me, Euthukles, and, hearted in each heart,
Athenai, undisgraced as Pallas' self,
Bear to my birthplace, Helios' island-bride,
Zeus' darling: thither speed us, homeward-bound,
Wafted already twelve hours' sail away
From horror, nearer by one sunset Rhodes!

Why should despair be? Since, distinct above
Man's wickedness and folly, flies the wind
And floats the cloud, free transport for our soul
Out of its fleshly durance dim and low,—
Since disembodied soul anticipates

(Thought-borne as now in rapturous unrestraint)
Above all crowding; crystal silentness,
Above all noise, a silver solitude:—
Surely, where thought so bears soul, soul in time
May permanently bide, "assert the wise,"
There live in peace, there work in hope once more—
Oh, nothing doubt, Philemon! Greed and strife,
Hatred and cark and care, what place have they
In yon blue liberality of heaven?
How the sea helps! How rose-smit earth will rise
Breast-high thence, some bright morning, and be Rhodes!
Heaven, earth and sea, my warrant—in their name,
Believe—o'er falsehood, truth is surely sphered,
O'er ugliness beams beauty, o'er this world
Extends that realm where "as the wise assert,"
Philemon, thou shalt see Euripides
Clearer than mortal sense perceived the man!

A sunset nearer Rhodes, by twelve hours' sweep
Of surge secured from horror? Rather say,
Quieted out of weakness into strength.
I dare invite, survey the scene my sense
Staggered to apprehend: for, disenvolved
From the mere outside anguish and contempt,
Slowly a justice centred in a doom
Reveals itself. Ay, pride succumbed to pride,
Oppression met the oppressor and was matched.
Athenai's vaunt braved Sparté's violence
Till, in the shock, prone fell Peiraios, low
Rampart and bulwark lay, as—timing stroke
Of hammer, axe, and beam hoist, poised and swung—
The very flute-girls blew their laughing best,
In dance about the conqueror while he bade
Music and merriment help enginery
Batter down, break to pieces all the trust
Of citizens once, slaves now. See what walls
Play substitute for the long double range
Themistoklean, heralding a guest
From harbor on to citadel! Each side
Their senseless walls demolished stone by stone,
See,—outer wall as stonelike, heads and hearts,—
Athenai's terror-stricken populace!
Prattlers, tongue-tied in crouching abjectness,—
Braggarts, who wring hands wont to flourish swords—
Sophist and rhetorician, demagogue,
(Argument dumb, authority a jest,)
Dikast and heliast, pleader, litigant,
Quack-priest, sham-prophecy-retailer, scout

O' the customs, sycophant, whate'er the style,
Altar-scrap-snatcher, pimp and parasite,—
Rivalities at truce now each with each,
Stupefied mud-banks,—such an use they serve!
While the one order which performs exact
To promise, functions faithful last as first,
What is it but the city's lyric troop,
Chantress and psaltress, flute-girl, dancing-girl?
Athenai's harlotry takes laughing care
Their patron miss no pipings, late she loved,
But deathward tread at least the kordax-step.

Die then, who pulled such glory on your heads!
There let it grind to powder! Perikles!
The living are the dead now: death be life!
Why should the sunset yonder waste its wealth?
Prove thee Olumpian! If my heart supply
Inviolate the structure,—true to type,
Build me some spirit-place no flesh shall find,
As Pheidias may inspire thee; slab on slab,
Renew Athenai, quarry out the cloud,
Convert to gold yon west extravagance!
'Neath Propulaia, from Akropolis
By vapory grade and grade, gold all the way,
Step to thy snow-Pnux, mount thy Bema-cloud,
Thunder and lighten thence a Hellas through
That shall be better and more beautiful
And too august for Sparté's foot to spurn!
Chasmed in the crag, again our Theatre
Predominates, one purple: Staghunt-month,
Brings it not Dionusia? Hail, the Three!
Aischulos, Sophokles, Euripides
Compete, gain prize or lose prize, godlike still.
Nay, lest they lack the old god-exercise—
Their noble want the unworthy,—as of old,
(How otherwise should patience crown their might?)
What if each find his ape promoted man,
His censor raised for antic service still?
Some new Hermippos to pelt Perikles,
Kratinos to swear Pheidias robbed a shrine,
Eruxis—I suspect, Euripides,
No brow will ache because with mop and mow
He gibes my poet! There 's a dog-faced dwarf
That gets to godship somehow, yet retains
His apehood in the Egyptian hierarchy,
More decent, indecorous just enough:
Why should not dog-ape, graced in due degree,
Grow Momos as thou Zeus? Or didst thou sigh

Rightly with thy Makaria? "After life,
Better no sentiency than turbulence;
Death cures the low contention." Be it so!
Yet progress means contention, to my mind.

Euthukles, who, except for love that speaks,
Art silent by my side while words of mine
Provoke that foe from which escape is vain
Henceforward, wake Athenai's fate and fall,—
Memories asleep as, at the altar-foot,
Those Furies in the Oresteian song,—
Do I amiss, who wanting strength use craft,
Advance upon the foe I cannot fly,
Nor feign a snake is dormant though it gnaw?
That fate and fall, once bedded in our brain,
Roots itself past upwrenching; but coaxed forth,
Encouraged out to practise fork and fang,—
Perhaps, when satiate with prompt sustenance,
It may pine, likelier die than if left swell
In peace by our pretension to ignore,
Or pricked to threefold fury, should our stamp
Bruise and not brain the pest.

        A middle course!
What hinders that we treat this tragic theme
As the Three taught when either woke some woe,
—How Klutaimnestra hated, what the pride
Of Iokasté, why Medeia clove
Nature asunder. Small rebuked by large,
We felt our puny hates refine to air,
Our poor prides sink, prevent the humbling hand,
Our petty passions purify their tide.
So, Euthukles, permit the tragedy
To re-enact itself, this voyage through,
Till sunsets end and sunrise brighten Rhodes!
Majestic on the stage of memory,
Peplosed and kothorned, let Athenai fall
Once more, nay, oft again till life conclude,
Lent for the lesson: Choros, I and thou!
What else in life seems piteous any more
After such pity, or proves terrible
Beside such terror?

        Still—since Phrunichos
Offended, by too premature a touch
Of that Milesian smart-place freshly frayed—
(Ah, my poor people, whose prompt remedy
Was—fine the poet, not reform thyself!)

Beware precipitate approach! Rehearse
Rather the prologue, well a year away,
Than the main misery, a sunset old.
What else but fitting prologue to the piece
Style an adventure, stranger than my first
By so much as the issue it enwombed
Lurked big beyond Balaustion's littleness?
Second supreme adventure! O that Spring,
That eve I told the earlier to my friends!
Where are the four now, with each red-ripe mouth
Crumpled so close, no quickest breath it fetched
Could disengage the lip-flower furled to bud
For fear Admetos—shivering head and foot,
As with sick soul and blind averted face
He trusted hand forth to obey his friend—
Should find no wife in her cold hand's response,
Nor see the disenshrouded statue start.
Alkestis, live the life and love the love!
I wonder, does the streamlet ripple still,
Out-smoothing galingale and watermint
Its mat-floor? while at brim, 'twixt sedge and sedge,
What bubblings past Baccheion, broadened much,
Pricked by the reed and fretted by the fly,
Oared by the boatman-spider's pair of arms!
Lenaia was a gladsome month ago—
Euripides had taught "Andromedé"
Next month, would teach "Kresphontes"—which same month
Some one from Phokis, who companioned me
Since all that happened on those temple-steps,
Would marry me and turn Athenian too.
Now! if next year the masters let the slaves
Do Bacchic service and restore mankind
That trilogy whereof, 'tis noised, one play
Presents the Bacchai,—no Euripides
Will teach the choros, nor shall we be tinged
By any such grand sunset of his soul,
Exiles from dead Athenai,—not the live
That's in the cloud there with the new-born star!

Speak to the infinite intelligence,
Sing to the everlasting sympathy!
Winds belly sail, and drench of dancing brine
Buffet our boat-side, so the prore bound free!
Condense our voyage into one great day
Made up of sunset-closes: eve by eve,
Resume that memorable night-discourse
When—like some meteor-brilliance, fire and filth,
Or say, his own Amphitheos, deity

And dung, who, bound on the gods' embassage,
Got men's acknowledgement in kick and cuff—
We made acquaintance with a visitor
Ominous, apparitional, who went
Strange as he came, but shall not pass away.
Let us attempt that memorable talk,
Clothe the adventure's every incident
With due expression: may not looks be told,
Gesture made speak, and speech so amplified
That words find blood-warmth which, cold-writ, they lose?

Recall the night we heard the news from Thrace,
One year ago, Athenai still herself.

We two were sitting silent in the house,
Yet cheerless hardly. Euthukles, forgive!
I somehow speak to unseen auditors.
Not you, but—Euthukles had entered, grave,
Grand, may I say, as who brings laurel-branch
And message from the tripod: such it proved.

He first removed the garland from his brow,
Then took my hand and looked into my face.

"Speak good words!" much misgiving faltered I.

"Good words, the best, Balaustion! He is crowned,
Gone with his Attic ivy home to feast,
Since Aischulos required companionship.
Pour a libation for Euripides!"

When we had sat the heavier silence out—
"Dead and triumphant still!" began reply
To my eye's question. "As he willed, he worked:
And, as he worked, he wanted not, be sure,
Triumph his whole life through, submitting work
To work's right judges, never to the wrong,
To competency, not ineptitude.
When he had run life's proper race and worked
Quite to the stade's end, there remained to try
The stade's turn, should strength dare the double course.
Half the diaulos reached, the hundred plays
Accomplished, force in its rebound sufficed
To lift along the athlete and ensure
A second wreath, proposed by fools for first,
The statist's olive as the poet's bay.
Wiselier, he suffered not a twofold aim
Retard his pace, confuse his sight; at once

Poet and statist; though the multitude
Girded him ever 'All thine aim thine art?
The idle poet only? No regard
For civic duty, public service, here?
We drop our ballot-bean for Sophokles!
Not only could he write "Antigoné"
But—since (we argued) whoso penned that piece
Might just as well conduct a squadron,—straight
Good-naturedly he took on him command.
Got laughed at, and went back to making plays,
Having allowed us our experiment
Respecting the fit use of faculty.'
No whit the more did athlete slacken pace.
Soon the jeers grew: 'Cold hater of his kind,
A sea-cave suits him, not the vulgar hearth!
What need of tongue-talk, with a bookish store
Would stock ten cities?' Shadow of an ass!
No whit the worse did athlete touch the mark
And, at the turning-point, consign his scorn
O' the scorners to that final trilogy
'Hupsipule,' 'Phoinissai,' and the Match
Of Life Contemplative with Active Life,
Zethos against Amphion. Ended so?
Nowise!—began again; for heroes rest
Dropping shield's oval o'er the entire man.
Ami he who thus took Contemplation's prize
Turned stade-point but to face Activity.
Out of all shadowy hands extending help
For life's decline pledged to youth's labor still,
Whatever renovation flatter age,—
Society with pastime, solitude
With peace,—he chose the hand that gave the heart,
Bade Macedonian Archelaos take
The leavings of Athenai, ash once flame.
For fifty politicians' frosty work,
One poet's ash proved ample and to spare:
He propped the state and filled the treasury,
Counselled the king as might a meaner soul,
Furnished the friend with what shall stand in stead
Of crown and sceptre, star his name about
When these are dust; for him, Euripides
Last the old hand on the old phorminx flung,
Clashed thence 'Alkaion,' maddened 'Pentheus' up;
Then music sighed itself away, one moan
Iphigeneia made by Aulis' strand;
With her and music died Euripides.

"The poet-friend who followed him to Thrace,

Agathon, writes thus much: the merchant-ship
Moreover brings a message from the king
To young Euripides, who went on board
This morning at Mounuchia: all is true."

I said "Thank Zeus for the great news and good!"

"Nay, the report is running in brief fire
Through the town's stubbly furrow," he resumed:
—"Entertains brightly what their favorite styles
'The City of Gapers' for a week perhaps,
Supplants three luminous tales, but yesterday
Pronounced sufficient lamps to last the month:
How Glauketes, outbidding Morsimos,
Paid market-price for one Kopaic eel
A thousand drachmai, and then cooked his prize
Not proper conger-fashion but in oil
And nettles, as man fries the foam-fish-kind;
How all the captains of the triremes, late
Victors at Arginousai, on return
Will, for return, be straightway put to death;
How Mikon wagered a Thessalian mime
Trained him by Lais, looked on as complete,
Against Leogoras' blood-mare koppa-marked,
Valued six talents,—swore, accomplished so,
The girl could swallow at a draught, nor breathe,
A choinix of unmixed Mendesian wine;
And having lost the match will—dine on herbs!
Three stories late aflame, at once extinct,
Outblazed by just 'Euripides is dead'!

"I met the concourse from the Theatre,
The audience flocking homeward: victory
Again awarded Aristophanes
Precisely for his old play chopped and changed,
'The Female Celebrators of the Feast'—
That Thesmophoria, tried a second time.
'Never such full success!'—assured the folk,
Who yet stopped praising to have word of mouth
With 'Euthukles, the bard's own intimate,
Balaustion's husband, the right man to ask.'

"'Dead, yes, but how dead, may acquaintance know?
You were the couple constant at his cave:
Tell us now, is it true that women, moved
By reason of his liking Krateros' ...

"I answered 'He was loved by Sokrates.'

"'Nay,' said another, 'envy did the work!
For, emulating poets of the place,
One Arridaios, one Krateues, both
Established in the royal favor, these' ...

"'Protagoras instructed him,' said I.

"'Phu,' whistled Comic Platon, 'hear the fact!
'Twas well said of your friend by Sophokles,
"He hate our women? In his verse, belike.
But when it comes to prose-work,—ha, ha, ha!"
New climes don't change old manners: so, it chanced,
Pursuing an intrigue one moonless night
With Arethousian Nikodikos' wife,
(Come now, his years were simply seventy-five,)
Crossing the palace-court, what haps he on
But Archelaos' pack of hungry hounds?
Who tore him piecemeal ere his cry brought help.'

"I asked: Did not you write 'The Festivals'?
You best know what dog tore him when alive.
You others, who now make a ring to hear,
Have not you just enjoyed a second treat,
Proclaimed that ne'er was play more worthy prize
Than this, myself assisted at, last year,
And gave its worth to,—spitting on the same?
Appraise no poetry,—price cuttlefish,
Or that seaweed-alphestes, scorpion-sort,
Much famed for mixing mud with fantasy
On midnights! I interpret no foul dreams."

If so said Euthukles, so could not I,
Balaustion, say. After "Lusistraté"
No more for me of "people's privilege,"
No witnessing "the Grand old Comedy
Coeval with our freedom, which, curtailed,
Were freedom's deathblow: relic of the past,
When Virtue laughingly told truth to Vice,
Uncensured, since the stern mouth, stuffed with flowers,
Through poetry breathed satire, perfumed blast
Which sense snuffed up while searched unto the bone!"
I was a stranger: "For first joy," urged friends,
"Go hear our Comedy, some patriot piece
That plies the selfish advocates of war
With argument so unevadable
That crash fall Kleons whom the finer play
Of reason, tickling, deeper wounds no whit

Than would a spear-thrust from a savory-stalk!
No: you hear knave and fool told crime and fault,
And see each scourged his quantity of stripes.
'Rough dealing, awkward language,' whine our fops:
The world's too squeamish now to bear plain words
Concerning deeds it acts with gust enough:
But, thanks to wine-lees and democracy,
We've still our stage where truth calls spade a spade!
Ashamed? Phuromachos' decree provides
The sex may sit discreetly, witness all,
Sorted, the good with good, the gay with gay,
Themselves unseen, no need to force a blush.
A Rhodian wife and ignorant so long?
Go hear next play!"

       I heard "Lusistraté."
Waves, said to wash pollution from the world,
Take that plague-memory, cure that pustule caught
As, past escape, I sat and saw the piece
By one appalled at Phaidra's fate,—the chaste,
Whom, because chaste, the wicked goddess chained
To that same serpent of unchastity
She loathed most, and who, coiled so, died distraught
Rather than make submission, loose one limb
Love-wards, at lambency of honeyed tongue,
Or torture of the scales which scraped her snow
—I say, the piece by him who charged this piece
(Because Euripides shrank not to teach,
If gods be strong and wicked, man, though weak,
May prove their match by willing to be good)
With infamies the Scythian's whip should cure—
"Such outrage done the public—Phaidra named!
Such purpose to corrupt ingenuous youth,
Such insult cast on female character!"—
Why, when I saw that bestiality—
So beyond all brute-beast imagining,
That when, to point the moral at the close,
Poor Salabaccho, just to show how fair
Was "Reconciliation," stripped her charms,
That exhibition simply bade us breathe,
Seemed something healthy and commendable
After obscenity grotesqued so much
It slunk away revolted at itself.
Henceforth I had my answer when our sage
Pattern-proposing seniors pleaded grave,
"You fail to fathom here the deep design!
All's acted in the interest of truth,
Religion, and those manners old and dear

Which made our city great when citizens
Like Aristeides and like Miltiades
Wore each a golden tettix in his hair."
What do they wear now under—Kleophon?

Well, for such reasons,—I am out of breath,
But loathsomeness we needs must hurry past,—
I did not go to see, nor then nor now,
The "Thesmophoriazousai." But, since males
Choose to brave first, blame afterward, nor brand
Without fair taste of what they stigmatize,
Euthukles had not missed the first display,
Original portrait of Euripides
By "Virtue laughingly reproving Vice:"
"Virtue,"—the author, Aristophanes,
Who mixed an image out of his own depths,
Ticketed as I tell you. Oh, this time
No more pretension to recondite worth!
No joke in aid of Peace, no demagogue
Pun-pelleted from Pnux, no kordax-dance
Overt helped covertly the Ancient Faith!
All now was muck, home-produce, honestman
The author's soul secreted to a play
Which gained the prize that day we heard the death.

I thought "How thoroughly death alters things!
Where is the wrong now, done our dead and great?
How natural seems grandeur in relief,
Cliff-base with frothy spites against its calm!"

Euthukles interposed—he read my thought—

"O'er them, too, in a moment came the change.
The crowd's enthusiastic, to a man:
Since, rake as such may please the ordure-heap
Because of certain sparkles presumed ore,
At first flash of true lightning overhead,
They look up, nor resume their search too soon.
The insect-scattering sign is evident,
And nowhere winks a firefly rival now,
Nor bustles any beetle of the brood
With trundled dung-ball meant to menace heaven.
Contrariwise, the cry is 'Honor him!'
'A statue in the theatre!' wants one;
Another 'Bring the poet's body back,
Bury him in Peiraios: o'er his tomb
Let Alkamenes carve the music-witch,
The songstress-siren, meed of melody:

Thoukudides invent his epitaph!'
To-night the whole town pays its tribute thus."

Our tribute should not be the same, my friend!
Statue? Within our heart he stood, he stands!
As for the vest outgrown now by the form,
Low flesh that clothed high soul,—a vesture's fate—
Why, let it fade, mix with the elements
There where it, falling, freed Euripides!
But for the soul that's tutelary now
Till time end, o'er the world to teach and bless—
How better hail its freedom than by first
Singing, we two, its own song back again,
Up to that face from which flowed beauty—face
Now abler to see triumph and take love
Than when it glorified Athenai once?

The sweet and strange Alkestis, which saved me,
Secured me—you, ends nowise, to my mind,
In pardon of Admetos. Hearts are fain
To follow cheerful weary Herakles
Striding away from the huge gratitude,
Club shouldered, lion-fleece round loin and flank,
Bound on the next new labor "height o'er height
Ever surmounting,—destiny's decree!"
Thither He helps us: that's the story's end;
He smiling said so, when I told him mine—
My great adventure, how Alkestis helped.
Afterward, when the time for parting fell,
He gave me, with two other precious gifts,
This third and best, consummating the grace,
"Herakles," writ by his own hand, each line.

"If it have worth, reward is still to seek.
Somebody, I forget who, gained the prize
And proved arch-poet: time must show!" he smiled:
"Take this, and, when the noise tires out, judge me—
Some day, not slow to dawn, when somebody—
Who? I forget—proves nobody at all!"

Is not that day come? What if you and I
Re-sing the song, inaugurate the fame?
We have not waited to acquaint ourselves
With song and subject; we can prologize
How, at Eurustheus' bidding,—hate strained hard,—
Herakles had departed, one time more,
On his last labor, worst of all the twelve;
Descended into Haides, thence to drag

The triple-headed hound, which sun should see
Spite of the god whose darkness whelped the Fear.
Down went the hero, "back—how should he come?"
So laughed King Lukos, an old enemy,
Who judged that absence testified defeat
Of the land's loved one,—since he saved the land
And for that service wedded Megara
Daughter of Thebai, realm her child should rule.
Ambition, greed and malice seized their prey,
The Heracleian House, defenceless left,
Father and wife and child, to trample out
Trace of its hearth-fire: since extreme old age
Wakes pity, woman's wrong wins championship,
And child may grow up man and take revenge.
Hence see we that, from out their palace-home
Hunted, for last resource they cluster now
Couched on the cold ground, hapless supplicants
About their court-yard altar,—Household Zeus
It is, the Three in funeral garb beseech,
Delaying death so, till deliverance come—
When did it ever?—from the deep and dark.
And thus breaks silence old Amphitruon's voice....
Say I not true thus far, my Euthukles?

Suddenly, torch-light! knocking at the door,
Loud, quick, "Admittance for the revels' lord!"
Some unintelligible Komos-cry—
Raw-flesh red, no cap upon his head,
Dionusos, Bacchos, Phales, Iacchos,
In let him reel with the kid-skin at his heel,
Where it buries in the spread of the bushy myrtle-bed!
(Our Rhodian Jackdaw-song was sense to that!)
Then laughter, outbursts ruder and more rude,
Through which, with silver point, a fluting pierced,
And ever "Open, open, Bacchos bids!"

But at last—one authoritative word,
One name of an immense significance:
For Euthukles rose up, threw wide the door.

There trooped the Choros of the Comedy
Crowned and triumphant; first, those flushed Fifteen,
Men that wore women's garb, grotesque disguise.
Then marched the Three,—who played Mnesilochos,
Who, Toxotes, and who, robed right, masked rare,
Monkeyed our Great and Dead to heart's content
That morning in Athenai. Masks were down
And robes doffed now; the sole disguise was drink.

Mixing with these—I know not what gay crowd,
Girl-dancers, flute-boys, and pre-eminent
Among them,—doubtless draped with such reserve
As stopped fear of the fifty-drachma fine
(Beside one's name on public fig-tree nailed)
Which women pay who in the streets walk bare,—
Behold Elaphion of the Persic dance!
Who lately had frisked fawn-foot, and the rest,
—All for the Patriot Cause, the Antique Faith,
The Conservation of True Poesy—
Could I but penetrate the deep design!
Elaphion, more Peiraios-known as "Phaps,"
Tripped at the head of the whole banquet-band
Who came in front now, as the first fell back;
And foremost—the authoritative voice,
The revels-leader, he who gained the prize,
And got the glory of the Archon's feast—
There stood in person Aristophanes.

And no ignoble presence! On the bulge
Of the clear baldness,—all his head one brow,—
True, the veins swelled, blue network, and there surged
A red from cheek to temple,—then retired
As if the dark-leaved chaplet damped a flame,—
Was never nursed by temperance or health.
But huge the eyeballs rolled back native fire,
Imperiously triumphant: nostrils wide
Waited their incense; while the pursed mouth's pout
Aggressive, while the beak supreme above,
While the head, face, nay, pillared throat thrown back,
Beard whitening tinder like a vinous foam,
These made a glory, of such insolence—
I thought,—such domineering deity
Hephaistos might have carved to cut the brine
For his gay brother's prow, imbrue that path
Which, purpling, recognized the conqueror.
Impudent and majestic: drunk, perhaps,
But that's religion; sense too plainly snuffed:
Still, sensuality was grown a rite.

What I had disbelieved most proved most true.
There was a mind here, mind a-wantoning
At ease of undisputed mastery
Over the body's brood, those appetites.
Oh, but he grasped them grandly, as the god
His either struggling handful,—hurtless snakes
Held deep down, strained hard off from side and side!

Mastery his, theirs simply servitude,
So well could firm fist help intrepid eye.
Fawning and fulsome, had they licked and hissed?
At mandate of one muscle, order reigned.
They had been wreathing much familiar now
About him on his entry; but a squeeze
Choked down the pests to place: their lord stood free.

Forward he stepped: I rose and fronted him.

"Hail, house, the friendly to Euripides!"
(So he began) "Hail, each inhabitant!
You, lady? What, the Rhodian? Form and face,
Victory's self upsoaring to receive
The poet? Right they named you ... some rich name,
Vowel-buds thorned about with consonants,
Fragrant, felicitous, rose-glow enriched
By the Isle's unguent: some diminished end
In ion, Kallistion? delicater still,
Kubelion or Melittion,—or, suppose
(Less vulgar love than bee or violet)
Phibalion, for the mouth split red-fig-wise,
Korakinidion for the coal-black hair,
Nettarion, Phabion for the darlingness?
But no, it was some fruit-flower, Rhoidion ... ha,
We near the balsam-bloom—Balaustion! Thanks,
Rhodes! Folk have called me Rhodian, do you know?
Not fools so far! Because, if Helios wived,
As Pindaros sings somewhere prettily,
Here blooms his offspring, earth-flesh with sun-fire,
Rhodes' blood and Helios' gold. My phorminx, boy!
Why does the boy hang back and balk an ode
Tiptoe at spread of wing? But like enough,
Sunshine frays torchlight. Witness whom you scare,
Superb Balaustion! Look outside the house!
Pho, you have quenched my Komos by first frown,
Struck dead all joyance: not a fluting puffs
From idle cheekband! Ah, my Choros too?
You've eaten cuckoo-apple? Dumb, you dogs?
So much good Thasian wasted on your throats
And out of them not one Threttanelo?
Neblaretai! Because this earth-and-sun
Product looks wormwood and all bitter herbs?
Well, do I blench, though me she hates the most
Of mortals? By the cabbage, off they slink!
You, too, my Chrusomelolonthion-Phaps,
Girl-goldling-beetle-beauty? You, abashed,
Who late, supremely unabashable,

Propped up my play at that important point
When Artamouxia tricks the Toxotes?
Ha, ha,—thank Hermes for the lucky throw,—
We came last comedy of the whole seven,
So went all fresh to judgment well-disposed
For who should fatly feast them, eye and ear,
We two between us! What, you fail your friend?
Away then, free me of your cowardice!
Go, get you the goat's breakfast! Fare afield,
Ye circumcised of Egypt, pigs to sow,
Back to the Priest's or forward to the crows,
So you but rid me of such company!
Once left alone, I can protect myself
From statuesque Balaustion pedestalled
On much disapprobation and mistake!
She dares not beat the sacred brow, beside!
Bacchos' equipment, ivy safeguards well
As Phoibos' bay.

       "They take me at my word!
One comfort is, I shall not want them long,
The Archon's cry creaks, creaks, 'Curtail expense!'
The war wants money, year the twenty-sixth!
Cut down our Choros number, clip costume,
Save birds' wings, beetles' armor, spend the cash
In three-crest skull-caps, three days' salt-fish-slice,
Three-banked-ships for these sham-ambassadors,
And what not: any cost but Comedy's!
'No Choros'—soon will follow; what care I?
Archinos and Agurrhios, scrape your flint,
Flay your dead dog, and curry favor so!
Choros in rags, with loss of leather next,
We lose the boys' vote, lose the song and dance,
Lose my Elaphion! Still, the actor stays.
Save but my acting, and the baldhead bard
Kudathenaian and Pandionid,
Son of Philippos, Aristophanes
Surmounts his rivals now as heretofore,
Though stinted to mere sober prosy verse—
'Manners and men,' so squeamish gets the world!
No more 'Step forward, strip for anapæsts!'
No calling naughty people by their names,
No tickling audience into gratitude
With chickpease, barleygroats and nuts and plums,
No setting Salabaccho" ...

      As I turned—

"True, lady, I am tolerably drunk:
The proper inspiration! Otherwise,—
Phrunichos, Choirilos!—had Aischulos
So foiled you at the goat-song? Drink 's a god.
How else did that old doating driveller
Kratinos foil me, match my masterpiece
The 'Clouds'? I swallowed cloud-distilment—dew
Undimmed by any grape-blush, knit my brow
And gnawed my style and laughed my learnedest;
While he worked at his 'Willow-wicker-flask,'
Swigging at that same flask by which he swore,
Till, sing and empty, sing and fill again,
Somehow result was—what it should not be
Next time, I promised him and kept my word!
Hence, brimful now of Thasian ... I 'll be bound,
Mendesian, merely: triumph-night, you know,
The High Priest entertains the conqueror,
And, since war worsens all things, stingily
The rascal starves whom he is bound to stuff,
Choros and actors and their lord and king
The poet: supper, still he needs must spread—
And this time all was conscientious fare:
He knew his man, his match, his master—made
Amends, spared neither fish, flesh, fowl nor wine:
So merriment increased, I promise you,
Till—something happened."

                Here he strangely paused,

"After that,—Well, it either was the cup
To the Good Genius, our concluding pledge,
That wrought me mischief, decently unmixed,—
Or, what if, when that happened, need arose
Of new libation? Did you only know
What happened! Little wonder I am drunk."

Euthukles, o'er the boat-side, quick, what change,
Watch, in the water! But a second since,
It laughed a ripply spread of sun and sea,
Say fused with wave, to never disunite.
Now, sudden all the surface, hard and black,
Lies a quenched light, dead motion: What the cause?
Look up and lo, the menace of a cloud
Has solemnized the sparkling, spoil the sport!
Just so, some overshadow, some new care
Stopped all the mirth and mocking on his face
And left there only such a dark surmise
—No wonder if the revel disappeared,

So did his face shed silence every side!
I recognized a new man fronting me.

"So!" he smiled, piercing to my thought at once,
"You see myself? Balaustion's fixed regard
Can strip the proper Aristophanes
Of what our sophists, in their jargon, style
His accidents? My soul sped forth but now
To meet your hostile survey,—soul unseen,
Yet veritably cinct for soul-defence
With satyr sportive quips, cranks, boss and spike,
Just as my visible body paced the street,
Environed by a boon companionship
Your apparition also puts to flight.
Well, what care I, if, unaccoutred twice,
I front my foe—no comicality
Round soul, and body-guard in banishment?
Thank your eyes' searching, undisguised I stand:
The merest female child may question me.
Spare not, speak bold, Balaustion!"

                    I did speak:

"Bold speech be—welcome to this honored hearth,
Good Genius! Glory of the poet, glow
O' the humorist who castigates his kind,
Suave summer-lightning lambency which plays
On stag-horned tree, misshapen crag askew,
Then vanishes with unvindictive smile
After a moment's laying black earth bare.
Splendor of wit that springs a thunderball—
Satire—to burn and purify the world,
True aim, fair purpose: just wit justly strikes
Injustice,—right, as rightly quells the wrong,
Finds out in knaves', fools', cowards' armory
The tricky tinselled place fire flashes through,
No damage else, sagacious of true ore;
Wit, learned in the laurel, leaves each wreath
O'er lyric shell or tragic barbiton,—
Though alien gauds be singed,—undesecrate,
The genuine solace of the sacred brow.
Ay, and how pulses flame a patriot-star
Steadfast athwart our country's night of things,
To beacon, would she trust no meteor-blaze,
Athenai from the rock she steers for straight!
O light, light, light, I hail light everywhere,
No matter for the murk that was,—perchance,
That will be,—certes, never should have been

Such orb's associate!

       "Aristophanes!
'The merest female child may question you?'
Once, in my Rhodes, a portent of the wave
Appalled our coast: for many a darkened day,
Intolerable mystery and fear.
Who snatched a furtive glance through crannied peak,
Could but report of snake-scale, lizard-limb,—
So swam what, making whirlpools as it went,
Madded the brine with wrath or monstrous sport.
"'T is Tuphon, loose, unmanacled from mount.'
Declared the priests, 'no way appeasable
Unless perchance by virgin-sacrifice!'
Thus grew the terror and o'erhung the doom—
Until one eve a certain female-child
Strayed in safe ignorance to seacoast edge,
And there sat down and sang to please herself.
When all at once, large-looming from his wave,
Out leaned, chin hand-propped, pensive on the ledge,
A sea-worn face, sad as mortality,
Divine with yearning after fellowship.
He rose but breast-high. So much god she saw;
So much she sees now, and does reverence!"

Ah, but there followed tail-splash, frisk of fin!
Let cloud pass, the sea's ready laugh outbreaks.
No very godlike trace retained the mouth
Which mocked with—

       "So, He taught you tragedy!
I always asked 'Why may not women act?'
Nay, wear the comic visor just as well;
Or, better, quite cast off the face-disguise
And voice-distortion, simply look and speak,
Real women playing women as men—men!
I shall not wonder if things come to that,
Some day when I am distant far enough.
Do you conceive the quite new Comedy
When laws allow? laws only let girls dance,
Pipe, posture,—above all, Elaphionize,
Provided they keep decent—that is, dumb.
Ay, and, conceiving, I would execute,
Had I but two lives: one were overworked!
How penetrate encrusted prejudice,
Pierce ignorance three generations thick
Since first Sousarion crossed our boundary?
He battered with a big Megaric stone;

Chionides felled oak and rough-hewed thence
This club I wield now, having spent my life
In planing knobs and sticking studs to shine;
Somebody else must try mere polished steel!"

Emboldened by the sober mood's return,
"Meanwhile," said I, "since planed and studded club
Once more has pashed competitors to dust,
And poet proves triumphant with that play
Euthukles found last year unfortunate,—
Does triumph spring from smoothness still more smoothed,
Fresh studs sown thick and threefold? In plain words,
Have you exchanged brute-blows,—which teach the brute
Man may surpass him in brutality,—
For human fighting, or true god-like force
Which breathes persuasion nor needs fight at all?
Have you essayed attacking ignorance,
Convicting folly, by their opposites,
Knowledge and wisdom? not by yours for ours,
Fresh ignorance and folly, new for old,
Greater for less, your crime for our mistake!
If so success at last have crowned desert,
Bringing surprise (dashed haply by concern
At your discovery such wild waste of strength
—And what strength!—went so long to keep in vogue
Such warfare—and what warfare!—shamed so fast,
So soon made obsolete, as fell their foe
By the first arrow native to the orb,
First onslaught worthy Aristophanes)—
Was this conviction's entry that same strange
'Something that happened' to confound your feast?"

"Ah, did he witness then my play that failed,
First 'Thesmophoriazousai'? Well and good!
But did he also see—your Euthukles—
My 'Grasshoppers,' which followed and failed too,
Three months since, at the 'Little-in-the-Fields'?"

"To say that he did see that First—should say
He never cared to see its following."

"There happens to be reason why I wrote
First play and second also. Ask the cause!
I warrant you receive, ere talk be done,
Fit answer, authorizing either act.
But here 's the point: as Euthukles made vow
Never again to taste my quality,
So I was minded next experiment

Should tickle palate—yea, of Euthukles!
Not by such utter change, such absolute
A topsyturvy of stage-habitude
As you and he want,—Comedy built fresh,
By novel brick and mortar, base to roof,—
No, for I stand too near and look too close!
Pleasure and pastime yours, spectators brave,
Should I turn art's fixed fabric upside down!
Little you guess how such tough work tasks soul!
Not overtasks, though: give fit strength fair play,
And strength 's a demiourgos! Art renewed?
Ay, in some closet where strength shuts out—first
The friendly faces, sympathetic cheer:
'More of the old provision, none supplies
So bounteously as thou,—our love, our pride,
Our author of the many a perfect piece!
Stick to that standard, change were decadence!
Next, the unfriendly: 'This time, strain will tire,
He 's fresh, Ameipsias thy antagonist!'
—Or better, in some Salaminian cave
Where sky and sea and solitude make earth
And man and noise one insignificance,
Let strength propose itself,—behind the world,—
Sole prize worth winning, work that satisfies
Strength it has dared and done strength's uttermost!
After which,—clap-to closet and quit cave,—
Strength may conclude in Archelaos' court,
And yet esteem the silken company
So much sky-scud, sea-froth, earth-thistledown,
For aught their praise or blame should joy or grieve.
Strength amid crowds as late in solitude
May lead the still life, ply the wordless task:
Then only, when seems need to move or speak,
Moving—for due respect, when statesmen pass,
(Strength, in the closet, watched how spiders spin!)
Speaking—when fashion shows intelligence,
(Strength, in the cave, oft whistled to the gulls!)
In short, has learnt first, practised afterwards!
Despise the world and reverence yourself,—
Why, you may unmake things and remake things,
And throw behind you, unconcerned enough,
What 's made or marred: 'you teach men, are not taught!'
So marches off the stage Euripides!

"No such thin fare feeds flesh and blood like mine,
No such faint fume of fancy sates my soul,
No such seclusion, closet, cave or court,
Suits either: give me Iostephanos

Worth making happy what coarse way she will—
O happy-maker, when her cries increase
About the favorite! 'Aristophanes!
More grist to mill, here 's Kleophon to grind!
He's for refusing peace, though Sparté cede
Even Dekeleia! Here 's Kleonumos
Declaring—though he threw away his shield,
He 'll thrash you till you lay your lyre aside!
Orestes bids mind where you walk of nights—
He wants your cloak as you his cudgelling.
Here 's, finally, Melanthios fat with fish,
The gormandizer-spendthrift-dramatist!
So, bustle! Pounce on opportunity!
Let fun a-screaming in Parabasis,
Find food for folk agape at either end,
Mad for amusement! Times grow better too,
And should they worsen, why, who laughs, forgets.
In no ease, venture boy-experiments!
Old wine 's the wine: new poetry drinks raw:
Two plays a season is your pledge, beside;
So, give us "Wasps" again, grown hornets mow!'"

Then he changed.

             "Do you so detect in me—
Brow-bald, chin-bearded, me, curved cheek, carved lip,
Or where soul sits and reigns in either eye—
What suits the—stigma, I say,—style say you,
Of 'Wine-lees-poet'? Bravest of buffoons,
Less blunt, than Telekleides, less obscene
Than Murtilos, Hermippos: quite a match
In elegance for Eupolis himself,
Yet pungent as Kratinos at his best?
Graced with traditional immunity
Ever since, much about my grandsire's time,
Some funny village-man in Megara,
Lout-lord and clown-king, used a privilege,
As due religious drinking-bouts came round,
To daub his phiz,—no, that was afterward,—
He merely mounted cart with mates of choice
And traversed country, taking house by house,
At night,—because of danger in the freak,—
Then hollaed 'Skin-flint starves his laborers!
Clench-fist stows figs away, cheats government!
Such an one likes to kiss his neighbor's wife,
And beat his own; while such another ... Boh!'
Soon came the broad day, circumstantial tale,
Dancing and verse, and there 's our Comedy,

There's Mullos, there 's Euetes, there 's the stock
I shall be proud to graft my powers upon!
Protected? Punished quite as certainly
When Archons pleased to lay down each his law,—
Your Morucheides-Surakosios sort,—
Each season, 'No more naming citizens,
Only abuse the vice, the vicious spare!
Observe, henceforth no Areopagite
Demean his rank by writing Comedy!'
(They one and all could write the 'Clouds' of course.)
'Needs must we nick expenditure, allow
Comedy half a choros, supper—none,
Times being hard, while applicants increase
For, what costs cash, the Tragic Trilogy.'
Lofty Tragedians! How they lounge aloof
Each with his Triad, three plays to my one,
Not counting the contemptuous fourth, the frank
Concession to mere mortal levity,
Satyric pittance tossed our beggar-world!
Your proud Euripides from first to last
Doled out some five such, never deigned us more!
And these—what curds and whey for marrowy wine!
That same Alkestis you so rave about
Passed muster with him for a Satyr-play,
The prig!—why trifle time with toys and skits
When he could stuff four ragbags sausage-wise
With sophistry, with bookish odds and ends,
Sokrates, meteors, moonshine, 'Life 's not Life,'
'The tongue swore, but unsworn the mind remains,'
And fifty such concoctions, crabtree-fruit
Digested while, head low and heels in heaven,
He lay, let Comics laugh—for privilege!
Looked puzzled on, or pityingly off,
But never dreamed of paying gibe by jeer,
Buffet by blow: plenty of proverb-pokes
At vice and folly, wicked kings, mad mobs!
No sign of wincing at my Comic lash,
No protest against infamous abuse,
Malignant censure,—naught to prove I scourged
With tougher thong-than leek-and-onion-plait!
If ever he glanced gloom, aggrieved at all,
The aggriever must be—Aischulos perhaps:
Or Sophokles he 'd take exception to.
—Do you detect in me—in me, I ask,
The man like to accept this measurement
Of faculty, contentedly sit classed
Mere Comic Poet—since I wrote 'The Birds'?"

I thought there might lurk truth in jest's disguise.

"Thanks!" he resumed, so quick to construe smile!
"I answered—in my mind—these gapers thus:
Since old wine 's ripe and new verse raw, you judge—
What if I vary vintage-mode and mix
Blossom with must, give nosegay to the brew,
Fining, refining, gently, surely, till
The educated taste turns unawares
From customary dregs to draught divine?
Then answered—with my lips: More 'Wasps' you want?
Come next year and I give you 'Grasshoppers'!
And 'Grasshoppers' I gave them,—last month's play.
They formed the Choros. Alkibiades,
No longer Triphales but Trilophos,
(Whom I called Darling-of-the-Summertime,
Born to be nothing else but beautiful
And brave, to eat, drink, love his life away)
Persuades the Tettix (our Autochthon-brood,
That sip the dew and sing on olive-branch
Above the ant-and-emmet populace)
To summon all who meadow, hill and dale
Inhabit—bee, wasp, woodlouse, dragonfly—
To band themselves against red nipper-nose
Stagbeetle, huge Taügetan (you guess—
Sparté) Athenai needs must battle with,
Because her sons are grown effeminate
To that degree—so morbifies their flesh
The poison-drama of Euripides,
Morals and music—there 's no antidote
Occurs save warfare which inspirits blood,
And brings us back perchance the blessed time
When (Choros takes up tale) our commonalty
Firm in primeval virtue, antique faith,
Ere earwig-sophist plagued or pismire-sage,
Cockered no noddle up with A, b, g,
Book-learning, logic-chopping, and the moon,
But just employed their brains on "Ruppapai,
Row, boys, munch barley-bread, and take your ease—
Mindful, however, of the tier beneath!'
Ah, golden epoch! while the nobler sort
(Such needs must study, no contesting that!)
Wore no long curls but used to crop their hair,
Gathered the tunic well about the ham,
Remembering 't was soft sand they used for seat
At school-time, while—mark this—the lesson long,
No learner ever dared to cross his legs!
Then, if you bade him take the myrtle-bough

And sing for supper—'t was some grave romaunt
How man of Mitulené, wondrous wise,
Jumped into hedge, by mortals quickset called,
And there, anticipating Oidipous,
Scratched out his eyes and scratched them in again.
None of your Phaidras, Augés, Kanakés,
To mincing music, turn, trill, tweedle-trash,
Whence comes that Marathon is obsolete!
Next, my Antistrophé was—praise of Peace:
Ah, could our people know what Peace implies!
Home to the farm and furrow! Grub one's vine,
Romp with one's Thratta, pretty serving-girl.
When wifie 's busy bathing! Eat and drink.
And drink and eat, what else is good in life?
Slice hare, toss pancake, gayly gurgle down
The Thasian grape in celebration due
Of Bacchos! Welcome, dear domestic rite,
When wife and sons and daughters, Thratta too,
Pour pea-soup as we chant delectably
In Bacchos reels, his tunic at his heels!
Enough, you comprehend,—I do at least!
Then,—be but patient,—the Parabasis!
Pray! For in that I also pushed reform.
None of the self-laudation, vulgar brag,
Vainglorious rivals cultivate so much!
No! If some merest word in Art's defence
Justice demanded of me,—never fear!
Claim was preferred, but dignifiedly.
A cricket asked a locust (winged, you know)
What he had seen most rare in foreign parts?
'I have flown far,' chirped he, 'North, East, South, West,
And nowhere heard of poet worth a fig
If matched with Bald-head here, Aigina's boast,
Who in this play bids rivalry despair
Past, present, and to come, so marvellous
His Tragic, Comic, Lyric excellence!
Whereof the fit reward were (not to speak
Of dinner every day at public cost
I' the Prutaneion) supper with yourselves,
My Public, best dish offered bravest bard!'
No more! no sort of sin against good taste!
Then, satire,—Oh, a plain necessity!
But I won't tell you: for—could I dispense
With one more gird at old Ariphrades?
How scorpion-like he feeds on human flesh—
Ever finds out some novel infamy
Unutterable, inconceivable,
Which all the greater need was to describe

Minutely, each tail-twist at ink-shed time ...
Now, what 's your gesture caused by? What you loathe,
Don't I loathe doubly, else why take such pains
To tell it you? But keep your prejudice!
My audience justified you! Housebreakers!
This pattern-purity was played and failed
Last Rural Dionusia—failed! for why?
Ameipsias followed with the genuine stuff.
He had been mindful to engage the Four—
Karkinos and his dwarf-crab-family—
Father and sons, they whirled like spinning-tops,
Choros gigantically poked his fun,
The boys' frank laugh relaxed the seniors' brow,
The skies re-echoed victory's acclaim,
Ameipsias gained his due, I got my dose
Of wisdom for the future. Purity?
No more of that next month, Athenai mine!
Contrive new cut of robe who will,—I patch
The old exomis, add no purple sleeve!
The Thesmophoriazousai, smartened up
With certain plaits, shall please, I promise you!

"Yes, I took up the play that failed last year,
And re-arranged things; threw adroitly in—
No Parachoregema—men to match
My women there already; and when these
(I had a hit at Aristullos here,
His plan how womankind should rule the roast)
Drove men to plough—'A-field, ye cribbed of cape!'
Men showed themselves exempt from service straight
Stupendously, till all the boys cried 'Brave!'
Then for the elders, I bethought me too,
Improved upon Mnesilochos' release
From the old bowman, board and binding-strap:
I made his son-in-law Euripides
Engage to put both shrewish wives away—
'Gravity,' one, the other 'Sophist-lore'—
And mate with the Bald Bard's hetairai twain—
'Goodhumor' and 'Indulgence:' on they tripped,
Murrhiné, Akalanthis,—'beautiful
Their whole belongings'—crowd joined choros there!
And while the Toxotes wound up his part
By shower of nuts and sweetmeats on the mob,
The woman-choros celebrated New
Kalligeneia, the frank last-day rite.
Brief, I was chairéd and caressed and crowned
And the whole theatre broke out a-roar,
Echoed my admonition—choros-cap—

Rivals of mine, your hands to your faces!
Summon no more the Muses, the Graces,
Since here by my side they have chosen their places!
And so we all flocked merrily to feast,—
I, my choragos, choros, actors, mutes
And flutes aforesaid, friends in crowd, no fear,
At the Priest's supper; and hilarity
Grew none the less that, early in the piece,
Ran a report, from row to row close-packed,
Of messenger's arrival at the Port
With weighty tidings, 'Of Lusandros' flight,'
Opined one; 'That Euboia penitent
Sends the Confederation fifty ships,'
Preferred another; while 'The Great King's Eye
Has brought a present for Elaphion here,
That rarest peacock Kompolakuthes!'
Such was the supposition of a third.
'No matter what the news,' friend Strattis laughed,
'It won't be worse for waiting: while each click
Of the klepsudra sets a shaking grave
Resentment in our shark's-head, boiled and spoiled
By this time: dished in Sphettian vinegar,
Silphion and honey, served with cocks'-brain-sauce!
So, swift to supper, Poet! No mistake,
This play; nor, like the unflavored "Grasshoppers,"
Salt without thyme!' Right merrily we supped,
Till—something happened.

                    "Out it shall, at last!

"Mirth drew to ending, for the cup was crowned
To the Triumphant!' Kleonclapper erst,
Now, Plier of a scourge Euripides
Fairly turns tail from, flying Attiké
For Makedonia's rocks and frosts and bears,
Where, furry grown, he growls to match the squeak
Of girl-voiced, crocus-vested Agathon!
Ha ha, he he!' When suddenly a knock—
Sharp, solitary, cold, authoritative.

"'Babaiax! Sokrates a-passing by,
A-peering in, for Aristullos' sake,
To put a question touching Comic Law?'
"No! Enters an old pale-swathed majesty,
Makes slow mute passage through two ranks as mute,
(Strattis stood up with all the rest, the sneak!)
Gray brow still bent on ground, upraised at length
When, our Priest reached, full front the vision paused.

"'Priest!'—the deep tone succeeded the fixed gaze—
'Thou carest that thy god have spectacle
Decent and seemly; wherefore, I announce
That, since Euripides is dead to-day,
My Choros, at the Greater Feast, next month,
Shall, clothed in black, appear ungarlanded!'

"Then the gray brow sank low, and Sophokles
Re-swathed him, sweeping doorward: mutely passed
'Twixt rows as mute, to mingle possibly
With certain gods who convoy age to port;
And night resumed him.

                    "When our stupor broke,
Chirpings took courage, and grew audible.

"'Dead—so one speaks now of Euripides!'
'Ungarlanded dance Choros, did he say?
I guess the reason: in extreme old age
No doubt such have the gods for visitants.
Why did he dedicate to Herakles
An altar else, but that the god, turned Judge,
Told him in dream who took the crown of gold?
He who restored Akropolis the theft,
Himself may feel perhaps a timely twinge
At thought of certain other crowns he filched
From—who now visits Herakles the Judge.
Instance "Medeia"! that play yielded palm
To Sophokles; and he again—to whom?
Euphorion! Why? Ask Herakles the Judge!'
'Ungarlanded, just means—economy!
Suppress robes, chaplets, everything suppress
Except the poet's present! An old tale
Put capitally by Trugaios—eh?
News from the world of transformation strange!
How Sophokles is grown Simonides,
And—aged, rotten—all the same, for greed
Would venture on a hurdle out to sea!
So jokes Philonides. Kallistratos
Retorts, Mistake! Instead of stinginess—
The fact is, in extreme decrepitude,
He has discarded poet and turned priest,
Priest of Half-Hero Alkon: visited
In his own house too by Asklepios' self,
So he avers. Meanwhile, his own estate
Lies fallow; Iophon 's the manager,—
Nay, touches up a play, brings out the same,

Asserts true sonship. See to what you sink
After your dozen-dozen prodigies!
Looking so old—Euripides seems young,
Born ten years later.'

       "'Just his tricky style!
Since, stealing first away, he wins first word
Out of good-natured rival Sophokles,
Procures himself no bad panegyric.
Had fate willed otherwise, himself were taxed
To pay survivor's-tribute,—harder squeezed
From anybody beaten first to last,
Than one who, steadily a conqueror,
Finds that his magnanimity is tasked
To merely make pretence and—beat itself!'

"So chirped the feasters though suppressedly.

"But I—what else do you suppose?—had pierced
Quite through friends' outside-straining, foes' mock-praise,
And reached conviction hearted under all.
Death's rapid line had closed a life's account,
And cut off, left unalterably clear
The summed-up value of Euripides.

"Well, it might be the Thasian! Certainly
There sang suggestive music in my ears;
And, through—what sophists style—the wall of sense
My eyes pierced: death seemed life and life seemed death,
Envisaged that way, now, which I, before,
Conceived was just a moon-struck mood. Quite plain
There re-insisted,—ay, each prim stiff phrase
Of each old play, my still-new laughing-stock,
Had meaning, well worth poet's pains to state,
Should life prove half true life's term,—death, the rest.
As for the other question, late so large,
Now all at once so little,—he or I,—
Which better comprehended playwright craft,—
There, too, old admonition took fresh point.
As clear recurred our last word-interchange
Two years since, when I tried with 'Ploutos.' 'Vain!'
Saluted me the cold grave-bearded bard—
'Vain, this late trial, Aristophanes!
None balks the genius with impunity!
You know what kind's the nobler, what makes grave
Or what makes grin: there 's yet a nobler still,
Possibly,—what makes wise, not grave,—and glad,
Not grinning: whereby laughter joins with tears,

Tragic and Comic Poet prove one power,
And Aristophanes becomes our Fourth—
Nay, greatest! Never needs the Art stand still,
But those Art leans on lag, and none like you,
Her strongest of supports, whose step aside
Undoes the march: defection checks advance
Too late adventured! See the "Ploutos" here!
This step decides your foot from old to new—
Proves you relinquish song and dance and jest,
Discard the beast, and, rising from all-fours,
Fain would paint, manlike, actual human life,
Make veritable men think, say and do.
Here 's the conception: which to execute,
Where 's force? Spent! Ere the race began, was breath
O' the runner squandered' on each friendly fool—
Wit-fireworks fizzed off while day craved no flame;
How should the night receive her due of fire
Flared out in Wasps and Horses, Clouds and Birds,
Prodigiously a-crackle? Rest content!
The new adventure for the novel man
Born to that next success myself foresee
In right of where I reach before I rest.
At end of a long course, straight all the way,
Well may there tremble somewhat into ken
The untrod path, clouds veiled from earlier gaze!
None may live two lives: I have lived mine through,
Die where I first stand still. You retrograde.
I leave my life's work. I compete with you,
My last with your last, my "Antiope"—
"Phoinissai"—with this "Ploutos"? No, I think!
Ever shall great and awful Victory
Accompany my life—in Maketis
If not Athenai. Take my farewell, friend!
Friend,—for from no consummate excellence
Like yours, whatever fault may countervail,
Do I profess estrangement: murk the marsh,
Yet where a solitary marble block
Blanches the gloom, there let the eagle perch!
You show—what splinters of Pentelikos,
Islanded by what ordure! Eagles fly,
Rest on the right place, thence depart as free;
But 'ware man's footstep, would it traverse mire
Untainted! Mire is safe for worms that crawl.'

"Balaustion! Here are very many words,
All to portray one moment's rush of thought,—
And much they do it! Still, you understand.
The Archon, the Feast-master, read their sum

And substance, judged the banquet-glow extinct,
So rose, discreetly if abruptly, crowned
The parting cup,—'To the Good Genius, then!'

"Up starts young Strattis for a final flash:
'Ay, the Good Genius! To the Comic Muse,
She who evolves superiority.
Triumph and joy from sorrow, unsuccess
And all that 's incomplete in human life;
Who proves such actual failure transient wrong,
Since out of body uncouth, halt and maimed—
Since out of soul grotesque, corrupt or blank—
Fancy, uplifted by the Muse, can flit
To soul and body, reinstate them Man:
Beside which perfect man, how clear we see
Divergency from type was earth's effect!
Escaping whence by laughter,—Fancy's feat,—
We right man's wrong, establish true for false,—
Above misshapen body, uncouth soul,
Reach the fine form, the clear intelligence—
Above unseemliness, reach decent law,—
By laughter: attestation of the Muse
That low-and-ugsome is not signed and sealed
Incontrovertibly man's portion here,
Or, if here,—why, still high-and-fair exists
In that ethereal realm where laughs our soul
Lift by the Muse. Hail thou her ministrant!
Hail who accepted no deformity
In man as normal and remediless,
But rather pushed it to such gross extreme
That, outraged, we protest by eye's recoil
The opposite proves somewhere rule and law!
Hail who implied, by limning Lamachos,
Plenty and pastime wait on peace, not war!
Philokleon—better bear a wrong than plead,
Play the litigious fool to stuff the mouth
Of dikast with the due three-obol fee!
The Paphlagonian—stick to the old sway
Of few and wise, not rabble-government!
Trugaios, Pisthetairos, Strepsiades,—
Why multiply examples? Hail, in fine,
The hero of each painted monster—so
Suggesting the unpictured perfect shape!
Pour out! A laugh to Aristophanes!'

"'Stay, my fine Strattis'—and I stopped applause—
'To the Good Genius—but the Tragic Muse!
She who instructs her poet, bids man's soul

Play man's part merely nor attempt the gods'
Ill-guessed of! Task humanity to height,
Put passion to prime use, urge will, unshamed
When will's last effort breaks in impotence!
No power forego, elude: no weakness,—plied
Fairly by power and will,—renounce, deny!
Acknowledge, in such miscalled weakness, strength
Latent: and substitute thus things for words!
Make man run life's race fairly,—legs and feet,
Craving no false wings to o'erfly its length!
Trust on, trust ever, trust to end—in truth!
By truth of extreme passion, utmost will,
Shame back all false display of either force—
Barrier about such strenuous heat and glow,
That cowardice shall shirk contending,—cant,
Pretension, shrivel at truth's first approach!
Pour to the Tragic Muse's ministrant
Who, as he pictured pure Hippolutos,
Abolished our earth's blot Ariphrades;
Who, as he drew Bellerophon the bold,
Proclaimed Kleonumos incredible;
Who, as his Theseus towered up man once more,
Made Alkibiades shrink boy again!
A tear—no woman's tribute, weak exchange
For action, water spent and heart's-blood saved—
No man's regret for greatness gone, ungraced
Perchance by even that poor meed, man's praise—
But some god's superabundance of desire,
Yearning of will to 'scape necessity,—
Love's overbrimming for self-sacrifice,
Whence good might be, which never else may be,
By power displayed, forbidden this strait sphere,—
Effort expressible one only way—
Such tear from me fall to Euripides!'

"The Thasian!—All, the Thasian, I account!

"Whereupon outburst the whole company
Into applause and—laughter, would you think?

"'The unrivalled one! How, never at a loss,
He turns the Tragic on its Comic side
Else imperceptible! Here 's death itself—
Death of a rival, of an enemy,—
Scarce seen as Comic till the master-touch
Made it acknowledge Aristophanes!
Lo, that Euripidean laurel-tree
Struck to the heart by lightning! Sokrates

Would question us, with buzz of "how" and "why,"
Wherefore the berry's virtue, the bloom's vice,
Till we all wished him quiet with his friend;
Agathon would compose an elegy,
Lyric bewailment fit to move a stone,
And, stones responsive, we might wince, 't is like;
Nay, with most cause of all to weep the least,
Sophokles ordains mourning for his sake
While we confess to a remorseful twinge:—
Suddenly, who but Aristophanes,
Prompt to the rescue, puts forth solemn hand,
Singles us out the tragic tree's best branch,
Persuades it groundward and, at tip, appends,
For votive-visor, Faun's goat-grinning face!
Back it flies, evermore with jest a-top,
And we recover the true mood, and laugh!"

"I felt as when some Nikias,—ninny-like
Troubled by sunspot-portent, moon-eclipse,—
At fault a little, sees no choice but sound
Retreat from foeman; and his troops mistake
The signal, and hail onset in the blast,
And at their joyous answer, alalé,
Back the old courage brings the scattered wits;
He wonders what his doubt meant, quick confirms
The happy error, blows the charge amain.
So I repaired things.

                    "'Both be praised,' thanked I.
'You who have laughed with Aristophanes,
You who wept rather with the Lord of Tears!
Priest, do thou, president alike o'er each,
Tragic and Comic function of the god,
Help with libation to the blended twain!
Either of which who serving, only serves—
Proclaims himself disqualified to pour
To that Good Genius—complex Poetry,
Uniting each god-grace, including both:
Which, operant for body as for soul,
Masters alike the laughter and the tears,
Supreme in lowliest earth, sublimest sky.
Who dares disjoin these,—whether he ignores
Body or soul, whichever half destroys,—
Maims the else perfect manhood, perpetrates
Again the inexpiable crime we curse—
Hacks at the Hermai, halves each guardian shape
Combining, nowise vainly, prominence
Of august head and enthroned intellect,

With homelier symbol of asserted sense,—
Nature's prime impulse, earthly appetite.
For, when our folly ventures on the freak,
Would fain abolish joy and fruitfulness,
Mutilate nature—what avails the Head
Left solitarily predominant,—
Unbodied soul,—not Hermes, both in one?
I, no more than our City, acquiesce
In such a desecration, but defend
Man's double nature—ay, wert thou its foe!
Could I once more, thou cold Euripides,
Encounter thee, in naught would I abate
My warfare, nor subdue my worst attack
On thee whose life-work preached "Raise soul, sink sense!
Evirate Hermes!"—would avenge the god,
And justify myself. Once face to face,
Thou, the argute and tricksy, shouldst not wrap,
As thine old fashion was, in silent scorn
The breast that quickened at the sting of truth,
Nor turn from me, as, if the tale be true,
From Lais when she met thee in thy walks,
And questioned why she had no rights as thou.
Not so shouldst thou betake thee, be assured,
To book and pencil, deign me no reply!
I would extract an answer from those lips
So closed and cold, were mine the garden-chance!
Gone from the world! Does none remain to take
Thy part and ply me with thy sophist-skill?
No sun makes proof of his whole potency
For gold and purple in that orb we view:
The apparent orb does little but leave blind
The audacious, and confused the worshipping;
But, close on orb's departure, must succeed
The serviceable cloud,—must intervene,
Induce expenditure of rose and blue,
Reveal what lay in him was lost to us.
So, friends, what hinders, as we homeward go,
If, privileged by triumph gained to-day,
We clasp that cloud our sun left saturate,
The Rhodian rosy with Euripides?
Not of my audience on my triumph-day,
She nor her husband! After the night's news
Neither will sleep but watch; I know the mood.
Accompany! my crown declares my right!'

"And here you stand with those warm golden eyes!

"In honest language, I am scarce too sure

Whether I really felt, indeed expressed
Then, in that presence, things I now repeat:
Nor half, nor any one word,—will that do?
Maybe, such eyes must strike conviction, turn
One's nature bottom upwards, show the base—
The live rock latent under wave and foam:
Superimposure these! Yet solid stuff
Will ever and anon, obeying star,
(And what star reaches rock-nerve like an eye?)
Swim up to surface, spout or mud or flame,
And find no more to do than sink as fast.

"Anyhow, I have followed happily
The impulse, pledged my Genius with effect,
Since, come to see you, I am shown—myself!"

I answered:

      "One of us declared for both
'Welcome the glory of Aristophanes.'
The other adds: and,—if that glory last,
Nor marsh-born vapor creep to veil the same,—
Once entered, share in our solemnity!
Commemorate, as we, Euripides!"

"What?" he looked round, "I darken the bright house?
Profane the temple of your deity?
That 's true! Else wherefore does he stand portrayed?
What Rhodian paint and pencil saved so much,
Beard, freckled face, brow—all but breath, I hope!
Come, that 's unfair: myself am somebody,
Yet my pictorial fame 's just potter's work,—
I merely figure on men's drinking-mugs!
I and the Flat-nose, Sophroniskos' son,
Oft make a pair. But what 's this lies below?
His table-book and graver, playwright's tool!
And lo, the sweet psalterion, strung and screwed,
Whereon he tried those le-é-é-é-és
And ke-é-é-é-és and turns and trills,
Lovely lark's tirra-lirra, lad's delight!
Aischulos' bronze-throat eagle-bark at blood
Has somehow spoiled my taste for twitterings!
With ... what, and did he leave you 'Herakles'?
The 'Frenzied Hero,' one unfractured sheet,
No pine-wood tablets smeared with treacherous wax—
Papuros perfect as e'er tempted pen!
This sacred twist of bay-leaves dead and sere
Must be that crown the fine work failed to catch,—

No wonder! This might crown 'Antiope.'
'Herakles' triumph? In your heart perhaps!
But elsewhere? Come now, I'll explain the case,
Show you the main mistake. Give me the sheet!"

I interrupted:

      "Aristophanes!
The stranger-woman sues in her abode—
'Be honored as our guest!' But, call it—shrine,
Then 'No dishonor to the Daimon!' bids
The priestess 'or expect dishonor's due!'
You enter fresh from your worst infamy,
Last instance of long outrage; yet I pause,
Withhold the word a-tremble on my lip,
Incline me, rather, yearn to reverence,—
So you but suffer that I see the blaze
And not the bolt,—the splendid fancy-fling,
Not the cold iron malice, the launched lie
Whence heavenly fire has withered; impotent,
Yet execrable, leave it 'neath the look
Of yon impassive presence! What he scorned,
His life long, need I touch, offend my foot,
To prove that malice missed its mark, that lie
Cumbers the ground, returns to whence it came?
I marvel, I deplore,—the rest be mute!
But, throw off hate's celestiality,—
Show me, apart from song-flash and wit-flame,
A mere man's hand ignobly clenched against
Yon supreme calmness,—and I interpose,
Such as you see me! Silk breaks lightning's blow!"
He seemed to scarce so much as notice me,
Aught I had spoken, save the final phrase:
Arrested there.

      "Euripides grown calm!
Calmness supreme means dead and therefore safe,"
He muttered; then more audibly began—

"Dead! Such must die! Could people comprehend!
There 's the unfairness of it! So obtuse
Are all: from Solon downward with his saw,
'Let none revile the dead,—no, though the son,
Nay, far descendant, should revile thyself!'—
To him who made Elektra, in the act
Of wreaking vengeance on her worst of foes,
Scruple to blame, since speech that blames insults
Too much the very villain life-released.

Now, I say, only after death, begins
That formidable claim,—immunity
Of faultiness from fault's due punishment!
The living, who defame me,—why, they live:
Fools,—I best prove them foolish by their life,
Will they but work on, lay their work by mine,
And wait a little, one Olympiad, say!
Then, where 's the vital force, mine froze beside?
The sturdy fibre, shamed my brittle stuff?
The school-correctness, sure of wise award
When my vagaries cease to tickle taste?
Where 's censure that must sink me, judgment big
Awaiting just the word posterity
Pants to pronounce? Time's wave breaks, buries—whom,
Fools, when myself confronts you four years hence?
But die, ere next Lenaia,—safely so
You 'scape me, slink with all your ignorance,
Stupidity and malice, to that hole
O'er which survivors croak 'Respect the dead!'
Ay, for I needs must! But allow me clutch
Only a carrion-handful, lend it sense,
(Mine, not its own, or could it answer me?)
And question, 'You, I pluck from hiding-place,
Whose cant was, certain years ago, my "Clouds"
Might last until the swallows came with Spring—
Whose chatter, "Birds" are unintelligible,
Mere psychologic puzzling: poetry?
List, the true lay to rock a cradle with!
O man of Mitulené, wondrous wise!'
—Would not I rub each face in its own filth
To tune of 'Now that years have come and gone,
How does the fact stand? What 's demonstrable
By time, that tries things?—your own test, not mine
Who think men are, were, ever will be fools,
Though somehow fools confute fools,—as these, you!
Don't mumble to the sheepish twos and threes
You cornered and called "audience!" face this me
Who know, and can, and—helped by fifty years—
Do pulverize you pygmies, then as now!'

"Ay, now as then, I pulverize the brood,
Balaustion! Mindful, from the first, where foe
Would hide head safe when hand had flung its stone,
I did not turn cheek and take pleasantry,
But flogged while skin could purple and flesh start,
To teach fools whom they tried conclusions with.
First face a-splutter at me got such splotch
Of prompt slab mud as, filling mouth to maw,

Made its concern thenceforward not so much
To criticise me as go cleanse itself.
The only drawback to which huge delight,—
(He saw it, how he saw it, that calm cold
Sagacity you call Euripides!)
—Why, 't is that, make a muckheap of a man,
There, pillared by your prowess, he remains,
Immortally immerded. Not so he!
Men pelted him but got no pellet back.
He reasoned, I 'll engage,—'Acquaint the world
Certain minuteness butted at my knee?
Dogface Eruxis, the small satirist,—
What better would the manikin desire
Than to strut forth on tiptoe, notable
As who so far up fouled me in the flank?'
So dealt he with the dwarfs: we giants, too,
Why must we emulate their pin-point play?
Render imperishable—impotence,
For mud throw mountains? Zeus, by mud unreached,—
Well, 't was no dwarf he heaved Olumpos at!"

My heart burned up within me to my tongue.

"And why must men remember, ages hence,
Who it was rolled down rocks, but refuse too—
Strattis might steal from! mixture-monument,
Recording what? 'I, Aristophanes,
Who boast me much inventive in my art,
Against Euripides thus volleyed muck
Because, in art, he too extended bounds.
I—patriot, loving peace and hating war,—
Choosing the rule of few, but wise and good,
Rather than mob-dictature, fools and knaves
However multiplied their mastery,—
Despising most of all the demagogue,
(Noisome air-bubble, buoyed up, borne along
By kindred breath of knave and fool below,
Whose hearts swell proudly as each puffing face
Grows big, reflected in that glassy ball,
Vacuity, just bellied out to break
And righteously bespatter friends the first,)
I loathing,—beyond less puissant speech
Than my own god-grand language to declare,—
The fawning, cozenage and calumny
Wherewith such favorite feeds the populace
That fan and set him flying for reward:—
I who, detecting what vice underlies
Thought's superstructure,—fancy's sludge and slime

'Twixt fact's sound floor and thought's mere surface-growth
Of hopes and fears which root no deeplier down
Than where all such mere fungi breed and bloat—
Namely, man's misconception of the God:—
I, loving, hating, wishful from my soul
That truth should triumph, falsehood have defeat,
—Why, all my soul's supremacy of power
Did I pour out in volley just on him
Who, his whole life long, championed every cause
I called my heart's cause, loving as I loved,
Hating my hates, spurned falsehood, championed truth,—
Championed truth not by flagellating foe
With simple rose and lily, gibe and jeer,
Sly wink of boon-companion o'er the bowze
Who, while he blames the liquor, smacks the lip,
Blames, doubtless, but leers condonation too,—
No, the balled fist broke brow like thunderbolt,
Battered till brain flew! Seeing which descent,
None questioned that was first acquaintanceship,
The avenger's with the vice he crashed through bone.
Still, he displeased me; and I turned from foe
To fellow-fighter, flung much stone, more mud,—
But missed him, since he lives aloof, I see.'
Pah! stop more shame, deep-cutting glory through,
Nor add, this poet, learned,—found no taunt
Tell like 'That other poet studies books!'
Wise,—cried 'At each attempt to move our hearts,
He uses the mere phrase of daily life!'
Witty,—'His mother was a herb-woman!'
Veracious, honest, loyal, fair and good,—
'It was Kephisophon who helped him write!'

"Whence,—oh the tragic end of Comedy!—
Balaustion pities Aristophanes.
For, who believed him? Those who laughed so loud?
They heard him call the sun Sicilian cheese!
Had he called true cheese—curd, would muscle move?
What made them laugh but the enormous lie?
'Kephisophon wrote "Herakles"'? ha, ha,
What can have stirred the wine-dregs, soured the soul,
And set a-lying Aristophanes?
Some accident at which he took offence!
The Tragic Master in a moody muse
Passed him unhailing, and it hurts—it hurts!
Beside, there 's license for the Wine-lees-song!'"

Blood burnt the cheekbone, each black eye flashed fierce.

"But this exceeds our license! Stay awhile—
That 's the solution! both are foreigners,
The fresh-come Rhodian lady, and her spouse
The man of Phokis: newly resident,
Nowise instructed—that explains it all!
No born and bred Athenian but would smile,
Unless frown seemed more fit for ignorance.
These strangers have a privilege!

        "You blame"
(Presently he resumed with milder mien)
"Both theory and practice—Comedy:
Blame her from altitudes the Tragic friend
Rose to, and upraised friends along with him,
No matter how. Once there, all 's cold and fine,
Passionless, rational; our world beneath
Shows (should you condescend to grace so much
As glance at poor Athenai) grimly gross—
A population which, mere flesh and blood,
Eats, drinks, and kisses, falls to fisticuffs,
Then hugs as hugely: speaks too as it acts,
Prodigiously talks nonsense,—townsmen needs
Must parley in their town's vernacular.
Such world has, of two courses, one to choose:
Unworld itself,—or else go blackening off
To its crow-kindred, leave philosophy
Her heights serene, fit perch for owls like you.
Now, since the world demurs to either course,
Permit me,—in default of boy or girl,
So they be reared Athenian, good and true,—
To praise what you most blame! Hear Art's defence!
I 'll prove our institution, Comedy,
Coeval with the birth of freedom, matched
So nice with our Republic, that its growth
Measures each greatness, just as its decline
Would signalize the downfall of the pair.
Our Art began when Bacchos ... never mind!
You and your master don't acknowledge gods:
'They are not, no, they are not!' well,—began
When the rude instinct of our race outspoke,
Found,—on recurrence of festivity
Occasioned by black mother-earth's good will
To children, as they took her vintage-gifts,—
Found—not the least of many benefits—
That wine unlocked the stiffest lip, and loosed
The tongue late dry and reticent of joke,
Through custom's gripe which gladness thrusts aside.
So, emulating liberalities,

Heaven joined with earth for that god's day at least,
Renewed man's privilege, grown obsolete,
Of telling truth nor dreading punishment.
Whereon the joyous band disguised their forms
With skins, beast-fashion, daubed each phiz with dregs,
Then hollaed 'Neighbor, you are fool, you—knave,
You—hard to serve, you—stingy to reward!'
The guiltless crowed, the guilty sunk their crest,
And good folk gained thereby, 't was evident.
Whence, by degrees, a birth of happier thought,
The notion came—not simply this to say,
But this to do—prove, put in evidence,
And act the fool, the knave, the harsh, the hunks,
Who did prate, cheat, shake fist, draw purse-string tight,
As crowd might see, which only heard before.

"So played the Poet, with his man of parts;
And all the others, found unqualified
To mount cart and be persons, made the mob,
Joined choros, fortified their fellows' fun,
Anticipated the community,
Gave judgment which the public ratified.
Suiting rough weapon doubtless to plain truth,
They flung, for word-artillery, why—filth;
Still, folks who wiped the unsavory salute
From visage, would prefer the mess, to wit—
Steel, poked through midriff with a civil speech,
As now the way is: then, the kindlier mode
Was—drub not stab, rib-roast not scarify!
So did Sousarion introduce, and so
Did I, acceding, find the Comic Art:
Club,—if I call it,—notice what 's implied!
An engine proper for rough chastisement,
No downright slaying: with impunity—
Provided crabtree, steeped in oily joke,
Deal only such a bruise as laughter cures.
I kept the gained advantage: stickled still
For club-law—stout fun and allowanced thumps:
Knocked in each knob a crevice to hold joke
As fig-leaf holds the fat-fry.

                    "Next, whom thrash?
Only the coarse fool and the clownish knave?
Higher, more artificial, composite
Offence should prove my prowess, eye and arm!
Not who robs henroost, tells of untaxed figs,
Spends all his substance on stewed ellops-fish,
Or gives a pheasant to his neighbor's wife:

No! strike malpractice that affects the State,
The common weal—intriguer or poltroon,
Venality, corruption, what care I
If shrewd or witless merely?—so the thing
Lay sap to aught that made Athenai bright
And happy, change her customs, lead astray
Youth or age, play the demagogue at Pnux,
The sophist in Palaistra, or—what 's worst,
As widest mischief,—from the Theatre
Preach innovation, bring contempt on oaths,
Adorn licentiousness, despise the Cult.
Are such to be my game? Why, then there wants
Quite other cunning than a cudgel-sweep!
Grasp the old stout stock, but new tip with steel
Each boss, if I would bray—no callous hide
Simply, but Lamachos in coat of proof,
Or Kleon cased about with impudence!
Shaft pushed no worse while point pierced sparkling so
That none smiled 'Sportive, what seems savagest,
—Innocuous anger, spiteless rustic mirth!'
Yet spiteless in a sort, considered well,
Since I pursued my warfare till each wound
Went through the mere man, reached the principle
Worth purging from Athenai. Lamachos?
No, I attacked war's representative;
Kleon? No, flattery of the populace;
Sokrates? No, but that pernicious seed
Of sophists whereby hopeful youth is taught
To jabber argument, chop logic, pore
On sun and moon, and worship Whirligig.
Oh, your tragedian, with the lofty grace,
Aims at no other and effects as much?
Candidly: what 's a polished period worth,
Filed curt sententiousness of loaded line,
When he who deals out doctrine, primly steps
From just that selfsame moon he maunders of,
And, blood-thinned by his pallid nutriment,
Proposes to rich earth-blood—purity?
In me, 't was equal-balanced flesh rebuked
Excess alike in stuff-guts Glauketes
Or starveling Chairephon; I challenged both,—
Strong understander of our common life,
I urged sustainment of humanity.
Whereas when your tragedian cries up Peace—
He 's silent as to cheese-cakes Peace may chew;
Seeing through rabble-rule, he shuts his eye
To what were better done than crowding Pnux—
That 's dance 'Threttanelo, the Kuklops drunk!'

"My power has hardly need to vaunt itself!
Opposers peep and mutter, or speak plain:
'No naming names in Comedy!' votes one,
'Nor vilifying live folk!' legislates
Another, 'urge amendment on the dead!'
'Don't throw away hard cash,' supplies a third,
'But crib from actor's dresses, choros-treats!'
Then Kleon did his best to bully me:
Called me before the Law Court: 'Such a play
Satirized citizens with strangers there,
Such other,'—why, its fault was in myself!
I was, this time, the stranger, privileged
To act no play at all,—Egyptian, I—
Rhodian or Kameirensian, Aiginete,
Lindian, or any foreigner he liked—
Because I can't write Attic, probably!
Go ask my rivals,—how they roughed my fleece,
And how, shorn pink themselves, the huddled sheep
Shiver at distance from the snapping shears!
Why must they needs provoke me?

                    "All the same,
No matter for my triumph, I foretell
Subsidence of the day-star: quench his beams?
No Aias e'er was equal to the feat
By throw of shield, tough-hided seven times seven,
'Twixt sky and earth! 't is dullards soft and sure
Who breathe against his brightest, here a sigh
And there a 'So let be, we pardon you!'
Till the minute mist hangs a block, has tamed
Noonblaze to 'twilight mild and equable,'
Vote the old women spinning out of doors.
Give me the earth-spasm, when the lion ramped
And the bull gendered in the brave gold flare!
Oh, you shall have amusement,—better still,
Instruction! no more horse-play, naming names,
Taxing the fancy when plain sense will serve!
Thearion, now, my friend who bakes you bread,
What 's worthier limning than his household life?
His whims and ways, his quarrels with the spouse,
And how the son, instead of learning knead
Kilikian loaves, brings heartbreak on his sire
By buying horseflesh branded San, each flank,
From shrewd Menippos who imports the ware:
While pretty daughter Kepphé too much haunts
The shop of Sporgilos the barber! brave!
Out with Thearion's meal-tub politics

In lieu of Pisthetairos, Strepsiades!
That 's your exchange? O Muse of Megara!
Advise the fools 'Feed babe on weasel-lap
For wild-boar's marrow, Cheiron's hero-pap,
And rear, for man—Ariphrades, mayhap!'
Yes, my Balaustion, yes, my Euthukles,
That 's your exchange,—who, foreigners in fact
And fancy, would impose your squeamishness
On sturdy health, and substitute such brat
For the right offspring of us Rocky Ones,
Because babe kicks the cradle,—crows, not mewls!

"Which brings me to the prime fault, poison-speck
Whence all the plague springs—that first feud of all
'Twixt me and you and your Euripides.
'Unworld the world,' frowns he, my opposite.
I cry, 'Life!' 'Death,' he groans, 'our better Life!'
Despise what is—the good and graspable,
Prefer the out of sight and in at mind,
To village-joy, the well-side violet-patch,
The jolly club-feast when our field 's in soak,
Roast thrushes, hare-soup, pea-soup, deep washed down
With Peparethian; the prompt paying off
That black-eyed brown-skinned country-flavored wench
We caught among our brushwood foraging:
On these look fig-juice, curdle up life's cream,
And fall to magnifying misery!
Or, if you condescend to happiness,
Why, talk, talk, talk about the empty name
While thing's self lies neglected 'neath your nose!
I need particular discourtesy
And private insult from Euripides
To render contest with him credible?
Say, all of me is outraged! one stretched sense,
I represent the whole Republic,—gods,
Heroes, priests, legislators, poets,—prone,
And pummelled into insignificance,
If will in him were matched with power of stroke.
For see what he has changed or hoped to change!
How few years since, when he began the fight,
Did there beat life indeed Athenai through!
Plenty and peace, then! Hellas thundersmote
The Persian. He himself had birth, you say,
That morn salvation broke at Salamis,
And heroes still walked earth. Themistokles—
Surely his mere back-stretch of hand could still
Find, not so lost in dark, Odusseus?—he
Holding as surely on to Herakles,—

Who touched Zeus, link by link, the unruptured chain!
Were poets absent? Aischulos might hail—
With Pindaros, Theognis,—whom for sire?
Homeros' self, departed yesterday!
While Hellas, saved and sung to, then and thus,—
Ah, people,—ah, lost antique liberty!
We lived, ourselves, undoubted lords of earth:
Wherever olives flourish, corn yields crop
To constitute our title—ours such land!
Outside of oil and breadstuff,—barbarism!
What need of conquest? Let barbarians starve!
Devote our whole strength to our sole defence,
Content with peerless native products, home,
Beauty profuse in earth's mere sights and sounds,
Such men, such women, and such gods their guard!
The gods? he worshipped best who feared them most,
And left their nature uninquired into,
—Nature? their very names! pay reverence,
Do sacrifice for our part, theirs would be
To prove benignantest of playfellows.
With kindly humanism they countenanced
Our emulation of divine escapes
Through sense and soul: soul, sense are made to use;
Use each, acknowledging its god the while!
Crush grape, dance, drink, indulge, for Bacchos' sake!
'T is Aphrodité's feast-day—frisk and fling,
Provided we observe our oaths, and house
Duly the stranger: Zeus takes umbrage else!
Ah, the great time—had I been there to taste!
Perikles, right Olumpian,—occupied
As yet with getting an Olumpos reared
Marble and gold above Akropolis,—
Wisely so spends what thrifty fools amassed
For cut-throat projects. Who carves Promachos?
Who writes the Oresteia?

        "Ah, the time!
For, all at once, a cloud has blanched the blue,
A cold wind creeps through the close vineyard-rank,
The olive-leaves curl, violets crisp and close
Like a nymph's wrinkling at the bath's first splash
On breast. (Your pardon!) There 's a restless change,
Deterioration. Larks and nightingales
Are silenced, here and there a gor-crow grim
Flaps past, as scenting opportunity.
Where Kimon passaged to the Boulé once,
A starveling crew, unkempt, unshorn, unwashed,
Occupy altar-base and temple-step,

Are minded to indoctrinate our youth!
How call these carrion kill-joys that intrude?
'Wise men,' their nomenclature! Prodikos—
Who scarce could, unassisted, pick his steps
From way Theseia to the Tripods' way,—
This empty noddle comprehends the sun,—
How he 's Aigina's bigness, wheels no whit
His way from east to west, nor wants a steed!
And here 's Protagoras sets wrongheads right,
Explains what virtue, vice, truth, falsehood mean,
Makes all we seemed to know prove ignorance
Yet knowledge also, since, on either side
Of any question, something is to say,
Nothing to 'stablish, all things to disturb!
And shall youth go and play at kottabos,
Leaving unsettled whether moon-spots breed?
Or dare keep Choes ere the problem 's solved—
Why should I like my wife who dislikes me?
'But sure the gods permit this, censure that?'
So tell them! straight the answer 's in your teeth:
'You relegate these points, then, to the gods?
What and where are they?' What my sire supposed,
And where yon cloud conceals them! 'Till they 'scape,
And scramble down to Leda, as a swan,
Europa, as a bull! why not as—ass
To somebody? Your sire was Zeus perhaps!
Either—away with such ineptitude!
Or, wanting energy to break your bonds,
Stick to the good old stories, think the rain
Is—Zeus distilling pickle through a sieve!
Think thunder 's thrown to break Theoros' head
For breaking oaths first! Meanwhile let ourselves
Instruct your progeny you prate like fools
Of father Zeus, who 's but the atmosphere,
Brother Poseidon, otherwise called—sea,
And son Hephaistos—fire and nothing else!
Over which nothings there 's a something still,
"Necessity," that rules the universe
And cares as much about your Choes-feast
Performed or intermitted, as you care
Whether gnats sound their trump from head or tail!'
When, stupefied at such philosophy,
We cry, 'Arrest the madmen, governor!
Pound hemlock and pour bull's-blood, Perikles!'
Would you believe? The Olumpian bends his brow,
Scarce pauses from his building! 'Say they thus?
Then, they say wisely. Anaxagoras,
I had not known how simple proves eclipse

But for thy teaching! Go, fools, learn like me!'

"Well, Zeus nods: man must reconcile himself,
So, let the Charon's-company harangue,
And Anaxagoras be—as we wish!
A comfort is in nature: while grass grows
And water runs, and sesame pricks tongue,
And honey from Brilesian hollow melts
On mouth, and Bacchis' flavorous lip beats both,
You will not be untaught life's use, young man?
Pho! My young man just proves that panniered ass
Said to have borne Youth strapped on his stout back,
With whom a serpent bargained, bade him swap
The priceless boon for—water to quench thirst!
What 's youth to my young man? In love with age,
He Spartanizes, argues, fasts and frowns,
Denies the plainest rules of life, long since
Proved sound; sets all authority aside,
Must simply recommence things, learn ere act,
And think out thoroughly how youth should pass—
Just as if youth stops passing, all the same!

"One last resource is left us—poetry!
'Vindicate nature, prove Plataian help,
Turn out, a thousand strong, all right and tight,
To save Sense, poet! Bang the sophist-brood
Would cheat man out of wholesome sustenance
By swearing wine is water, honey—gall,
Saperdion—the Empousa! Panic-smit,
Our juveniles abstain from Sense and starve:
Be yours to disenchant them! Change things back!
Or better, strain a point the other way
And handsomely exaggerate wronged truth!
Lend wine a glory never gained from grape,
Help honey with a snatch of him we style
The Muses' Bee, baybloom-fed Sophokles,
And give Saperdion a Kimberic robe!'

"'I, his successor,' gruff the answer grunts,
'Incline to poetize philosophy,
Extend it rather than restrain; as thus—
Are heroes men? No more, and scarce as much,
Shall mine be represented. Are men poor?
Behold them ragged, sick, lame, halt and blind!
Do they use speech? Ay, street-terms, market-phrase!
Having thus drawn sky earthwards, what comes next
But dare the opposite, lift earth to sky?
Mere puppets once, I now make womankind,

For thinking, saying, doing, match the male.
Lift earth? I drop to, dally with, earth's dung!
—Recognize in the very slave—man's mate,
Declare him brave and honest, kind and true,
And reasonable as his lord, in brief.
I paint men as they are—so runs my boast—
Not as they should be: paint—what 's part of man,
—Women and slaves,—not as, to please your pride,
They should be, but your equals, as they are.
Oh, and the Gods! Instead of abject mien,
Submissive whisper, while my Choros cants,
"Zeus,—with thy cubit's length of attributes,—
May I, the ephemeral, ne'er scrutinize
Who made the heaven and earth and all things there!"
Myself shall say ... Ay, 'Herakles' may help!
Give me,—I want the very words,—attend!"

He read. Then—"Murder 's out,—'There are no Gods,'
Man has no master, owns, by consequence,
No right, no wrong, except to please or plague!
His nature: what man likes be man's sole law
Still, since he likes Saperdion, honey, figs,
Man may reach freedom by your roundabout!
'Never believe yourselves the freer thence!
There are no gods, but there 's "Necessity,"—
Duty enjoined you, fact in figment's place,
Throned on no mountain, native to the mind!
Therefore deny yourselves Saperdion, figs
And honey, for the sake of—what I dream,
A-sitting with my legs up!'

          "Infamy!
The poet casts in calm his lot with these
Assailants of Apollon! Sworn to serve
Each Grace, the Furies call him minister—
He, who was born for just that roseate world
Renounced so madly, where what 's false is fact,
Where he makes beauty out of ugliness,
Where he lives, life itself disguised for him
As immortality—so works the spell,
The enthusiastic mood which marks a man
Muse-mad, dream-drunken, wrapt around by verse,
Encircled with poetic atmosphere,
As lark emballed by its own crystal song,
Or rose enmisted by that scent it makes!
No, this were unreality! the real
He wants, not falsehood,—truth alone he seeks,
Truth, for all beauty! Beauty, in all truth—

That 's certain somehow! Must the eagle lilt
Lark-like, needs fir-tree blossom rose-like? No!
Strength and utility charm more than grace,
And what 's most ugly proves most beautiful.
So much assistance from Euripides!

"Whereupon I betake me, since needs must,
To a concluding—'Go and feed the crows!
Do! Spoil your art as you renounce your life,
Poetize your so precious system, do,
Degrade the hero, nullify the god,
Exhibit women, slaves and men as peers,—
Your castigation follows prompt enough!
When all 's concocted upstairs, heels o'erhead,
Down must submissive drop the masterpiece
For public praise or blame: so, praise away,
Friend Sokrates, wife's-friend Kephisophon!
Boast innovations, cramp phrase, uncouth song,
Hard matter and harsh manner, gods, men, slaves
And women jumbled to a laughing-stock
Which Hellas shall hold sides at lest she split!
Hellas, on these, shall have her word to say!'

"She has it and she says it—there 's the curse!—
She finds he makes the shag-rag hero-race,
The noble slaves, wise women, move as much
Pity and terror as true tragic types:
Applauds inventiveness—the plot so new,
The turn and trick subsidiary so strange!
She relishes that homely phrase of life,
That common town-talk, more than trumpet-blasts;
Accords him right to chop and change a myth:
What better right had he, who told the tale
In the first instance, to embellish fact?
This last may disembellish yet improve!
Both find a block: this man carves back to bull
What first his predecessor cut to sphinx:
Such genuine actual roarer, nature's brute,
Intelligible to our time, was sure
The old-world artist's purpose, had he worked
To mind; this both means and makes the thing!
If, past dispute, the verse slips oily-bathed
In unctuous music—say, effeminate—
We also say, like Kuthereia's self,
A lulling effluence which enswathes some isle
Where hides a nymph, not seen but felt the more.
That 's Hellas' verdict!

"Does Euripides
Even so far absolved, remain content?
Nowise! His task is to refine, refine,
Divide, distinguish, subtilize away
Whatever seemed a solid planting-place
For footfall,—not in that phantasmal sphere
Proper to poet, but on vulgar earth
Where people used to tread with confidence.
There 's left no longer one plain positive
Enunciation incontestable
Of what is good, right, decent here on earth.
Nobody now can say, 'This plot is mine,
Though but a plethron square,—my duty!'—'Yours?
Mine, or at least not yours,' snaps somebody!
And, whether the dispute be parent-right
Or children's service, husband's privilege
Or wife's submission, there 's a snarling straight,
Smart passage of opposing 'yea' and 'nay,'
'Should,' 'should not,' till, howe'er the contest end,
Spectators go off sighing 'Clever thrust!
Why was I so much hurried to pay debt,
Attend my mother, sacrifice an ox,
And set my name down "for a trireme, good"?
Something I might have urged on t' other side!
No doubt, Chresphontes or Bellerophon
We don't meet every day; but Stab-and-stitch
The tailor—ere I turn the drachmas o'er
I owe him for a chiton, as he thinks,
I 'll pose the blockhead with an argument!'

"So has he triumphed, your Euripides!
Oh, I concede, he rarely gained a prize:
That 's quite another matter! cause for that!
Still, when 't was got by Ions, Iophons,
Off he would pace confoundedly superb,
Supreme, no smile at movement on his mouth
Till Sokrates winked, whispered: out it broke!
And Aristullos jotted down the jest,
While Iophons or Ions, bay on brow,
Looked queerly, and the foreigners—like you—
Asked o'er the border with a puzzled smile,
—'And so, you value Ions, Iophons,
Euphorions! How about Euripides?'
(Eh, brave bard's-champion? Does the anger boil?
Keep within bounds a moment,—eye and lip
Shall loose their doom on me, their fiery worst!)
What strangers? Archelaos heads the file!
He sympathizes, he concerns himself,

He pens epistle, each successless play:
'Athenai sinks effete; there 's younger blood
In Makedonia. Visit where I rule!
Do honor to me and take gratitude!
Live the guest's life, or work the poet's way,
Which also means the statesman's: he who wrote
"Erechtheus" may seem rawly politic
At home where Kleophon is ripe; but here
My council-board permits him choice of seats.'

"Now, this was operating,—what should prove
A poison-tree, had flowered far on to fruit
For many a year,—when I was moved, first man,
To dare the adventure, down with root and branch.
So, from its sheath I drew my Comic steel,
And dared what I am now to justify.
A serious question first, though!

                "Once again!
Do you believe, when I aspired in youth,
I made no estimate of power at all,
Nor paused long, nor considered much, what class
Of fighters I might claim to join, beside
That class wherewith I cast in company?
Say, you—profuse of praise no less than blame—
Could not I have competed—franker phrase
Might trulier correspond to meaning—still,
Competed with your Tragic paragon?
Suppose me minded simply to make verse,
To fabricate, parade resplendent arms,
Flourish and sparkle out a Trilogy,—
Where was the hindrance? But my soul bade 'Fight!
Leave flourishing for mock-foe, pleasure-time;
Prove arms efficient on real heads and hearts!'
How? With degeneracy sapping fast
The Marathonian muscle, nerved of old
To maul the Mede, now strung at best to help
—How did I fable?—War and Hubbub mash
To mincemeat Fatherland and Brotherhood,
Pound in their mortar Hellas, State by State,
That greed might gorge, the while frivolity
Rubbed hands and smacked lips o'er the dainty dish!
Authority, experience—pushed aside
By any upstart who pleads throng and press,
O' the people! 'Think, say, do thus!' Wherefore, pray?
'We are the people: who impugns our right
Of choosing Kleon that tans hide so well,
Huperbolos that turns out lamps so trim,

Hemp-seller Eukrates or Lusikles
Sheep-dealer, Kephalos the potter's son,
Diitriphes who weaves the willow-work
To go round bottles, and Nausikudes
The meal-man? Such we choose and more, their mates,
To think and say and do in our behalf!'
While sophistry wagged tongue, emboldened still,
Found matter to propose, contest, defend,
'Stablish, turn topsyturvy,—all the same,
No matter what, provided the result
Were something new in place of something old,—
Set wagging by pure insolence of soul
Which needs must pry into, have warrant for
Each right, each privilege good policy
Protects from curious eye and prating mouth!
Everywhere lust to shape the world anew,
Spurn this Athenai as we find her, build
A new impossible Cloudcuckooburg
For feather-headed birds, once solid men,
Where rules, discarding jolly habitude,
Nourished on myrtle-berries and stray ants,
King Tereus who, turned Hoopoe Triple-Crest,
Shall terrify and bring the gods to terms!

"Where was I? Oh! Things ailing thus—I ask,
What cure? Cut, thrust, hack, hew at heap-on-heaped
Abomination with the exquisite
Palaistra-tool of polished Tragedy?
Erechtheus shall harangue Amphiktuon,
And incidentally drop word of weight
On justice, righteousness, so turn aside
The audience from attacking Sicily!—
The more that Choros, after he recounts
How Phrixos rode the ram, the far-famed Fleece,
Shall add—at last fall of grave dancing-foot—
'Aggression never yet was helped by Zeus!'
That helps or hinders Alkibiades?
As well expect, should Pheidias carve Zeus' self
And set him up, some half a mile away,
His frown would frighten sparrows from your field!
Eagles may recognize their lord, belike,
But as for vulgar sparrows,—change the god,
And plant some big Priapos with a pole!
I wield the Comic weapon rather—hate!
Hate! honest, earnest, and directest hate—
Warfare wherein I close with enemy,
Call him one name and fifty epithets,
Remind you his great-grandfather sold bran,

Describe the new exomion, sleeveless coat
He knocked me down last night and robbed me of,
Protest he voted for a tax on air!
And all this hate—if I write Comedy—
Finds tolerance, most like—applause, perhaps
True veneration; for I praise the god
Present in person of his minister,
And pay—the wilder my extravagance—
The more appropriate worship to the Power
Adulterous, night-roaming, and the rest:
Otherwise,—that originative force
Of nature, impulse stirring death to life,
Which, underlying law, seems lawlessness,
Yet is the outbreak which, ere order be,
Must thrill creation through, warm stocks and stones,
Phales Iacchos.

       "Comedy for me!
Why not for you, my Tragic masters? Sneaks
Whose art is mere desertion of a trust!
Such weapons lay to hand, the ready club,
The clay-ball, on the ground a stone to snatch,—
Arms fit to bruise the boar's neck, break the chine
O' the wolf,—and you must impiously—despise?
No, I 'll say, furtively let fall that trust
Consigned you! 'T was not 'take or leave alone,'
But 'take and, wielding, recognize your god
In his prime attributes!' And though full soon
You sneaked, subsided into poetry,
Nor met your due reward, still,—heroize
And speechify and sing-song and forego
Far as you may your function,—still its pact
Endures, one piece of early homage still
Exacted of you; after your three bouts
At hoitytoity, great men with long words,
And so forth,—at the end, must tack itself
The genuine sample, the Satyric Play,
Concession, with its wood-boys' fun and freak,
To the true taste of the mere multitude.
Yet, there again! What does your Still-at-itch,
Always-the-innovator? Shrugs and shirks!
Out of his fifty Trilogies, some five
Are somehow suited: Satyrs dance and sing,
Try merriment, a grimly prank or two,
Sour joke squeezed through pursed lips and teeth on edge,
Then quick on top of toe to pastoral sport,
Goat-tending and sheep-herding, cheese and cream,
Soft grass and silver rillets, country-fare—

When throats were promised Thasian! Five such feats,—
Then frankly off he threw the yoke: next Droll,
Next festive drama, covenanted fun,
Decent reversion to indecency,
Proved—your 'Alkestis'! There 's quite fun enough,
Herakles drunk! From out fate's blackening wave
Calamitous, just zigzags some shot star,
Poor promise of faint joy, and turns the laugh
On dupes whose fears and tears were all in waste!

"For which sufficient reasons, in truth's name,
I closed with whom you count the Meaner Muse,
Classed me with Comic Poets who should weld
Dark with bright metal, show their blade may keep
Its adamantine birthright though ablaze
With poetry, the gold, and wit, the gem,
And strike mere gold, unstiffened out by steel,
Or gem, no iron joints its strength around,
From hand of—posturer, not combatant!

"Such was my purpose: it succeeds, I say!
Have not we beaten Kallikratidas,
Not humbled Sparté? Peace awaits our word,
Spite of Theramenes, and fools his like.
Since my previsions—warranted too well
By the long war now waged and worn to end—
Had spared such heritage of misery,
My after-counsels scarce need fear repulse.
Athenai, taught prosperity has wings,
Cages the glad recapture. Demos, see,
From folly's premature decrepitude
Boiled young again, emerges from the stew
Of twenty-five years' trouble, sits and sways,
One brilliance and one balsam,—sways and sits
Monarch of Hellas! ay, and, sage again,
No longer jeopardizes chieftainship,
No longer loves the brutish demagogue
Appointed by a bestial multitude,
But seeks out sound advisers. Who are they?
Ourselves, of parentage proved wise and good!
To such may hap strains thwarting quality,
(As where shall want its flaw mere human stuff?)
Still, the right grain is proper to right race;
What 's contrary, call curious accident!
Hold by the usual! Orchard-grafted tree,
Not wilding, racehorse-sired, not rouncey-born,
Aristocrat, no sausage-selling snob!
Nay, why not Alkibiades, come back

Filled by the Genius, freed of petulance,
Frailty,—mere youthfulness that 's all at fault,—
Advanced to Perikles and something more?
—Being at least our duly born and bred,—
Curse on what chaunoprockt first gained his ear
And got his ... well, once true man in right place,
Our commonalty soon content themselves
With doing just what they are born to do,
Eat, drink, make merry, mind their own affairs
And leave state-business to the larger brain!
I do not stickle for their punishment;
But certain culprits have a cloak to twitch,
A purse to pay the piper: flog, say I,
Your fine fantastics, paragons of parts,
Who choose to play the important! Far from side
With us, their natural supports, allies,—
And, best by brain, help who are best by birth
To fortify each weak point in the wall
Built broad and wide and deep for permanence
Between what 's high and low, what 's rare and vile,—
They cast their lot perversely in with low
And vile, lay flat the barrier, lift the mob
To dizzy heights where Privilege stood firm.
And then, simplicity become conceit,—
Woman, slave, common soldier, artisan,
Crazy with new-found worth, new-fangled claims,—
These must be taught next how to use their heads
And hands in driving man's right to mob's rule!
What fellows thus inflame the multitude?
Your Sokrates, still crying 'Understand!'
Your Aristullos,—'Argue!' Last and worst,
Should, by good fortune, mob still hesitate,
Remember there 's degree in heaven and earth,
Cry 'Aischulos enjoined us fear the gods,
And Sophokles advised respect the kings!'
Why, your Euripides informs them—Gods?
They are not! Kings? They are, but ... do not I,
In 'Suppliants,' make my Theseus,—yours, no more,—
Fire up at insult of who styles him King?
Play off that Herald, I despise the most,
As patronizing kings' prerogative
Against a Theseus proud to dare no step
Till he consult the people?

        "Such as these—
Ah, you expect I am for strangling straight?
Nowise, Balaustion! All my roundabout
Ends at beginning, with my own defence!

I dose each culprit just with—Comedy.
Let each be doctored in exact the mode
Himself prescribes: by words, the word-monger—
My words to his words,—my lies, if you like,
To his lies. Sokrates I nickname thief,
Quack, necromancer; Aristullos,—say,
Male Kirké who bewitches and bewrays
And changes folk to swine; Euripides,—
Well, I acknowledge! Every word is false,
Looked close at; but stand distant and stare through,
All 's absolute indubitable truth
Behind lies, truth which only lies declare!
For come, concede me truth 's in thing not word,
Meaning not manner! Love smiles 'rogue' and 'wretch'
When 'sweet' and 'dear' seem vapid; Hate adopts
Love's 'sweet' and 'dear,' when 'rogue' and 'wretch' fall flat;
Love, Hate—are truths, then, each, in sense not sound.
Further: if Love, remaining Love, fell back
On 'sweet' and 'dear,'—if Hate, though Hate the same,
Dropped down to 'rogue' and 'wretch,'—each phrase were false.
Good! and now grant I hate no matter whom
With reason: I must therefore fight my foe,
Finish the mischief which made enmity.
How? By employing means to most hurt him
Who much harmed me. What way did he do harm?
Through word or deed? Through word? with word, wage war!
Word with myself directly? As direct
Reply shall follow: word to you, the wise,
Whence indirectly came the harm to me?
What wisdom I can muster waits on such!
Word to the populace which, misconceived
By ignorance and incapacity,
Ends in no such effect as follows cause
When I, or you the wise, are reasoned with,
So damages what I and you hold dear?
In that event, I ply the populace
With just such word as leavens their whole lump
To the right ferment for my purpose. They
Arbitrate properly between us both?
They weigh my answer with his argument,
Match quip with quibble, wit with eloquence?
All they attain to understand is—blank!
Two adversaries differ; which is right
And which is wrong, none takes on him to say,
Since both are unintelligible. Pooh!
Swear my foe's mother vended herbs she stole,
They fall a-laughing! Add,—his household drudge
Of all-work justifies that office well,

Kisses the wife, composing him the play,—
They grin at whom they gaped in wonderment,
And go off—'Was he such a sorry scrub?
This other seems to know! we praised too fast!'
When then, my lies have done the work of truth,
Since 'scrub,' improper designation, means
Exactly what the proper argument
—Had such been comprehensible—proposed
To proper audience—were I graced with such—
Would properly result in; so your friend
Gets an impartial verdict on his verse,
'The tongue swears, but the soul remains unsworn!'

"There, my Balaustion! All is summed and said.
No other cause of quarrel with yourself!
Euripides and Aristophanes
Differ: he needs must round our difference
Into the mob's ear; with the mob I plead.
You angrily start forward 'This to me?'
No speck of this on you the thrice refined!
Could parley be restricted to us two,
My first of duties were to clear up doubt
As to our true divergence each from each.
Does my opinion so diverge from yours?
Probably less than little—not at all!
To know a matter, for my very self
And intimates—that 's one thing: to imply
By 'knowledge'—loosing whatsoe'er I know
Among the vulgar who, by mere mistake,
May brain themselves and me in consequence,—
That 's quite another. 'O the daring flight!
This only bard maintains the exalted brow,
Nor grovels in the slime nor fears the gods!'
Did I fear—I play superstitious fool,
Who, with the due proviso, introduced,
Active and passive, their whole company
As creatures too absurd for scorn itself?
Zeus? I have styled him—'slave, mere thrashing-block!'
I 'll tell you: in my very next of plays,
At Bacchos' feast, in Bacchos' honor, full
In front of Bacchos' representative.
I mean to make main-actor—Bacchos' self!
Forth shall he strut, apparent, first to last,
A blockhead, coward, braggart, liar, thief,
Demonstrated all these by his own mere
Xanthias the man-slave: such man shows such god
Shamed to brute-beastship by comparison!
And when ears have their fill of his abuse,

And eyes are sated with his pummelling,—
My Choros taking care, by, all the while
Singing his glory, that men recognize
A god in the abused and pummelled beast,—
Then, should one ear be stopped of auditor,
Should one spectator shut revolted eye,—
Why, the Priest's self will first raise outraged voice:
'Back, thou barbarian, thou ineptitude!
Does not most license hallow best our day,
And least decorum prove its strictest rite?
Since Bacchos bids his followers play the fool,
And there 's no fooling like a majesty
Mocked at,—who mocks the god, obeys the law—
Law which, impute but indiscretion to,
And ... why, the spirit of Euripides
Is evidently active in the world!'
Do I stop here? No! feat of flightier force!
See Hermes! what commotion raged,—reflect!—
When imaged god alone got injury
By drunkards' frolic! How Athenai stared
Aghast, then fell to frenzy, fit on fit,—
Ever the last, the longest! At this hour,
The craze abates a little: so, my Play
Shall have up Hermes: and a Karion, slave,
(Since there 's no getting lower) calls our friend
The profitable god, we honor so,
Whatever contumely fouls the mouth—
Bids him go earn more honest livelihood
By washing tripe in well-trough—wash he does,
Duly obedient! Have I dared my best?
Asklepios, answer!—deity in vogue,
Who visits Sophokles familiarly,
If you believe the old man,—at his age,
Living is dreaming, and strange guests haunt door
Of house, belike, peep through and tap at times
When a friend yawns there, waiting to be fetched,—
At any rate, to memorize the fact,
He has spent money, set an altar up
In the god's temple, now in much repute.
That temple-service trust me to describe—
Cheaters and choused, the god, his brace of girls,
Their snake, and how they manage to snap gifts
'And consecrate the same into a bag,'
For whimsies done away with in the dark!
As if, a stone's throw from that theatre
Whereon I thus unmask their dupery,
The thing were not religious and august!

"Of Sophokles himself—nor word nor sign
Beyond a harmless parody or so!
He founds no anti-school, upsets no faith,
But, living, lets live, the good easy soul
Who,—if he saves his cash, unpoetlike,
Loves wine and—never mind what other sport,
Boasts for his father just a swordblade-smith,
Proves but queer captain when the people claim,
For one who conquered with 'Antigone,'
The right to undertake a squadron's charge,—
And needs the son's help now to finish plays,
Seeing his dotage calls for governance
And Iophon to share his property,—
Why, of all this, reported true, I breathe
Not one word—true or false, I like the man!
Sophokles lives and lets live: long live he!
Otherwise,—sharp the scourge and hard the blow!

"And what 's my teaching but—accept the old,
Contest the strange! acknowledge work that 's done,
Misdoubt men who have still their work to do!
Religions, laws and customs, poetries,
Are old? So much achieved victorious truth!
Each work was product of a lifetime, wrung
From each man by an adverse world: for why?
He worked, destroying other older work
Which the world loved and so was loth to lose.
Whom the world beat in battle—dust and ash!
Who beat the world, left work in evidence,
And wears its crown till new men live new lives,
And fight new fights, and triumph in their turn.
I mean to show you on the stage! you 'll see
My Just Judge only venture to decide
Between two suitors, which is god, which man,
By thrashing both of them as flesh can bear.
You shall agree,—whichever bellows first,
He 's human; who holds longest out, divine:
That is the only equitable test!
Cruelty? Pray, who pricked them on to court
My thong's award? Must they needs dominate?
Then I—rebel! Their instinct grasps the new?
Mine bids retain the old: a fight must be,
And which is stronger the event will show.
Oh, but the pain! Your proved divinity
Still smarts all reddened? And the rightlier served!
Was not some man's-flesh in him, after all?
Do let us lack no frank acknowledgment
There 's nature common to both gods and men!

All of them—spirit? What so winced was clay!
Away pretence to some exclusive sphere
Cloud-nourishing a sole selected few
Fume-fed with self-superiority!
I stand up for the common coarse-as-clay
Existence,—stamp and ramp with heel and hoof
On solid vulgar life, you fools disown!
Make haste from your unreal eminence,
And measure lengths with me upon that ground
Whence this mud-pellet sings and summons you!
I know the soul, too, how the spark ascends
And how it drops apace and dies away.
I am your poet-peer, man thrice your match!
I too can lead an airy life when dead,
Fly like Kinesias when I 'm cloud-ward bound;
But here, no death shall mix with life it mars!

"So, my old enemy who caused the fight,
Own I have beaten you, Euripides!
Or,—if your advocate would contravene,—
Help him, Balaustion! Use the rosy strength!
I have not done my utmost,—treated you
As I might Aristullos, mint-perfumed,—
Still, let the whole rage burst in brave attack!
Don't pay the poor ambiguous compliment
Of fearing any pearl-white knuckled fist
Will damage this broad buttress of a brow!
Fancy yourself my Aristonumos,
Ameipsias or Sannurion: punch and pound!
Three cuckoos who cry 'cuckoo'! much I care!
They boil a stone! Neblaretai! Rattei!"

Cannot your task have end here, Euthukles?
Day by day glides our galley on its path:
Still sunrise and still sunset, Rhodes half-reached,
And still, my patient scribe! no sunset's peace
Descends more punctual than that brow's incline
O'er tablets which your serviceable hand
Prepares to trace. Why treasure up, forsooth,
These relics of a night that make me rich,
But, half-remembered merely, leave so poor
Each stranger to Athenai and her past?
For—how remembered! As some greedy hind
Persuades a honeycomb, beyond the due,
To yield its hoarding,—heedless what alloy
Of the poor bee's own substance taints the gold
Which, unforced, yields few drops, but purity,—

So would you fain relieve of load this brain,
Though the hived thoughts must bring away, with strength,
What words and weakness, strength's receptacle—
Wax from the store! Yet,—aching soothed away,—
Accept the compound! No suspected scent
But proves some rose was rifled, though its ghost
Scarce lingers with what promised musk and myrrh.
No need of farther squeezing! What remains
Can only be Balaustion, just her speech!

Ah, but—because speech serves a purpose still!—

He ended with that flourish. I replied:

"Fancy myself your Aristonumos?
Advise me, rather, to remain myself,
Balaustion,—mindful what mere mouse confronts
The forest-monarch Aristophanes!
I who, a woman, claim no quality
Beside the love of all things lovable
Created by a power pre-eminent
In knowledge, as in love I stand perchance,
—You, the consummately-creative! How
Should I, then, dare deny submissive trust
To any process aiming at result
Such as you say your songs are pregnant with?
Result, all judge: means, let none scrutinize
Save those aware how glory best is gained
By daring means to end, ashamed of shame,
Constant in faith that only good works good,
While evil yields no fruit but impotence!
Graced with such plain good, I accept the means!
Nay, if result itself in turn become
Means,—who shall say?—to ends still loftier yet,—
Though still the good prove hard to understand,
The bad still seemingly predominate,—
Never may I forget which order bears
The burden, toils to win the great reward,
And finds, in failure, the grave punishment,
So, meantime, claims of me a faith I yield!
Moreover, a mere woman, I recoil
From what may prove man's-work permissible,
Imperative. Rough strokes surprise: what then?
Some lusty armsweep needs must cause the crash
Of thorn and bramble, ere those shrubs, those flowers,
We fain would have earth yield exclusively,
Are sown, matured and garlanded for boys
And girls, who know not how the growth was gained.

Finally, am I not a foreigner?
No born and bred Athenian,—isled about,
I scarce can drink, like you, at every breath,
Just some particular doctrine which may best
Explain the strange thing I revolt against—
How—by involvement, who may extricate?—
Religion perks up through impiety,
Law leers with license, folly wise-like frowns,
The seemly lurks inside the abominable.
But opposites,—each neutralizes each
Haply by mixture: what should promise death,
May haply give the good ingredient force,
Disperse in fume the antagonistic ill.
This institution, therefore,—Comedy,—
By origin, a rite; by exercise,
Proved an achievement tasking poet's power
To utmost, eking legislation out
Beyond the legislator's faculty,
Playing the censor where the moralist
Declines his function, far too dignified
For dealing with minute absurdities;
By efficacy,—virtue's guard, the scourge
Of vice, each folly's fly-flap, arm in aid
Of all that 's righteous, customary, sound
And wholesome; sanctioned therefore,—better say,
Prescribed for fit acceptance of this age
By, not alone the long recorded roll
Of earlier triumphs, but, success to-day—
(The multitude as prompt recipient still
Of good gay teaching from that monitor
They crowned this morning—Aristophanes—
As when Sousarion's car first traversed street)—
This product of Athenai—I dispute,
Impugn? There 's just one only circumstance
Explains that! I, poor critic, see, hear, feel;
But eyes, ears, senses prove me—foreigner!
Who shall gainsay that the raw new-come guest
Blames oft, too sensitive? On every side
Of—larger than your stage—life's spectacle,
Convention here permits and there forbids
Impulse and action, nor alleges more
Than some mysterious 'So do all, and so
Does no one:' which the hasty stranger blames
Because, who bends the head unquestioning,
Transgresses, turns to wrong what else were right,
By failure of a reference to law
Beyond convention; blames unjustly, too—
As if, through that defect, all gained were lost

And slave-brand set on brow indelibly;—
Blames unobservant or experienceless
That men, like trees, if stout and sound and sane,
Show stem no more affected at the root
By bough's exceptional submissive dip
Of leaf and bell, light danced at end of spray
To windy fitfulness in wayward sport,—
No more lie prostrate,—than low files of flower
Which, when the blast goes by, unruffled raise
Each head again o'er ruder meadow-wreck
Of thorn and thistle that refractory
Demurred to cower at passing wind's caprice.
Why shall not guest extend like charity,
Conceive how,—even when astounded most
That natives seem to acquiesce in muck
Changed by prescription, they affirm, to gold,—
Such may still bring to test, still bear away
Safely and surely much of good and true
Though latent ore, themselves unspecked, unspoiled?
Fresh bathed i' the icebrook, any hand may pass
A placid moment through the lamp's fierce flame:
And who has read your 'Lemnians,' seen 'The Hours,'
Heard 'Female-Playhouse-seat-Preoccupants,'
May feel no worse effect than, once a year,
Those who leave decent vesture, dress in rags
And play the mendicant, conform thereby
To country's rite, and then, no beggar-taint
Retained, don vesture due next morrow-day.
What if I share the stranger's weakness then?
Well, could I also show his strength, his sense
Untutored, ay!—but then untampered with!

"I fancy, though the world seems old enough,
Though Hellas be the sole unbarbarous land,
Years may conduct to such extreme of age,
And outside Hellas so isles new may lurk,
That haply,—when and where remain a dream!—
In fresh days when no Hellas fills the world,
In novel lands as strange where, all the same,
Their men and women yet behold, as we,
Blue heaven, black earth, and love, hate, hope and fear.
Over again, unhelped by Attiké—
Haply some philanthropic god steers bark,
Gift-laden, to the lonely ignorance
Islanded, say, where mist and snow mass hard
To metal—ay, those Kassiterides!
Then asks: 'Ye apprehend the human form.
What of this statue, made to Pheidias' mind,

This picture, as it pleased our Zeuxis paint?
Ye too feel truth, love beauty: judge of these!'
Such strangers may judge feebly, stranger-like:
'Each hair too indistinct—for, see our own!
Hands, not skin-colored as these hands we have,
And lo, the want of due decorum here!
A citizen, arrayed in civic garb,
Just as he walked your streets apparently,
Yet wears no sword by side, adventures thus,
In thronged Athenai! foolish painter's-freak!
While here 's his brother-sculptor found at fault
Still more egregiously, who shames the world,
Shows wrestler, wrestling at the public games,
Atrociously exposed from head to foot!'
Sure, the Immortal would impart at once
Our slow-stored knowledge, how small truths suppressed
Conduce to the far greater truth's display,—
Would replace simple by instructed sense,
And teach them how Athenai first so tamed
The natural fierceness that her progeny
Discarded arms nor feared the beast in man:
Wherefore at games, where earth's wise gratitude,
Proved by responsive culture, claimed the prize
For man's mind, body, each in excellence,—
When mind had bared itself, came body's turn,
And only irreligion grudged the gods
One naked glory of their master-work
Where all is glorious rightly understood,—
The human frame; enough that man mistakes:
Let him not think the gods mistaken too!

"But, peradventure, if the stranger's eye
Detected ... Ah, too high my fancy-flight!
Pheidias, forgive, and Zeuxis bear with me—
How on your faultless should I fasten fault
Of my own framing, even? Only say,—
Suppose the impossible were realized,
And some as patent incongruity,
Unseemliness,—of no more warrant, there
And then, than now and here, whate'er the time
And place,—I say, the Immortal,—who can doubt?—
Would never shrink, but own, 'The blot escaped
Our artist: thus he shows humanity!'

"May stranger tax one peccant part in thee,
Poet, three-parts divine! May I proceed?

"'Comedy is prescription and a rite.'

Since when? No growth of the blind antique time,
'It rose in Attiké with liberty;
When freedom falls, it too will fall.' Scarce so!
Your games,—the Olumpian, Zeus gave birth to these;
Your Puthian,—these were Phoibos' institute.
Isthmian, Nemeian,—Theseus, Herakles
Appointed each, the boys and barbers say!
Earth's day is growing late: where 's Comedy?
'Oh, that commenced an age since,—two, belike,—
In Megara, whence here they brought the thing!'
Or I misunderstand, or here 's the fact—
Your grandsire could recall that rustic song,
How such-an-one was thief, and miser such,
And how,—immunity from chastisement
Once promised to bold singers of the same
By daylight on the drunkard's holiday,—
The clever fellow of the joyous troop
Tried acting what before he sang about,
Acted and stole, or hoarded, acting too:
While his companions ranged a-row, closed up
For Choros,—bade the general rabblement
Sit, see, hear, laugh,—not join the dance themselves.
Soon, the same clever fellow found a mate,
And these two did the whole stage-mimicking,
Still closer in approach to Tragedy,—
So led the way to Aristophanes,
Whose grandsire saw Sousarion, and whose sire—
Chionides; yourself wrote 'Banqueters'
When Aischulos had made 'Prometheus,' nay,
All of the marvels; Sophokles,—I 'll cite,
'Oidipous'—and Euripides—I bend
The head—'Medeia' henceforth awed the world!
'Banqueters,' 'Babylonians'—next come you!
Surely the great days that left Hellas free
Happened before such advent of huge help,
Eighty-years-late assistance? Marathon,
Plataia, Salamis were fought, I think,
Before new educators stood reproved,
Or foreign legates blushed, excepted to!
Where did the helpful rite pretend its rise?
Did it break forth, as gifts divine are wont,
Plainly authentic, incontestably
Adequate to the helpful ordinance?
Founts, dowered with virtue, pulse out pure from source;
'T is there we taste the god's benign intent:
Not when,—fatigued away by journey, foul
With brutish trampling,—crystal sinks to slime,
And lymph forgets the first salubriousness.

Sprang Comedy to light thus crystal-pure?
'Nowise!' yourself protest with vehemence;
'Gross, bestial, did the clowns' diversion break;
Every successor paddled in the slush;
Nay, my contemporaries one and all
Gay played the mudlark till I joined their game;
Then was I first to change buffoonery
For wit, and stupid filth for cleanly sense,
Transforming pointless joke to purpose fine,
Transfusing rude enforcement of home-law—
"Drop knave's-tricks, deal more neighbor-like, ye boors!"—
With such new glory of poetic breath
As, lifting application far past use
O' the present, launched it o'er men's lowly heads
To future time, when high and low alike
Are dead and done with, while my airy power
Flies disengaged, as vapor from what stuff
It—say not, dwelt in—fitlier, dallied with
To forward work, which done,—deliverance brave,—
It soars away, and mud subsides to dust.
Say then, myself invented Comedy!'

"So mouths full many a famed Parabasis!
Agreed! No more, then, of prescriptive use,
Authorization by antiquity,
For what offends our judgment! 'T is your work,
Performed your way: not work delivered you
Intact, intact producible in turn.
Everywhere have you altered old to new—
Your will, your warrant: therefore, work must stand
Or stumble by intrinsic worth. What worth?
Its aim and object! Peace you advocate,
And war would fain abolish from the land:
Support religion, lash irreverence,
Yet laughingly administer rebuke
To superstitious folly,—equal fault!
While innovating rashness, lust of change,
New laws, new habits, manners, men and things,
Make your main quarry,—'oldest' meaning 'best.'
You check the fretful litigation-itch,
Withstand mob-rule, expose mob-flattery,
Punish mob-favorites; most of all press hard
On sophists who assist the demagogue,
And poets their accomplices in crime.
Such your main quarry,—by the way, you strike
Ignobler game, mere miscreants, snob or scamp,
Cowardly, gluttonous, effeminate:
Still with a bolt to spare when dramatist

Proves haply unproficient in his art,
Such aims—alone, no matter for the means—
Declare the unexampled excellence
Of their first author—Aristophanes!

"Whereat—Euripides, oh, not thyself—
Augustlier than the need!—thy century
Of subjects dreamed and dared and done, before
'Banqueters' gave dark earth enlightenment,
Or 'Babylonians' played Prometheus here,—
These let me summon to defend thy cause!
Lo, as indignantly took life and shape
Labor by labor, all of Herakles,—
Palpably fronting some o'erbold pretence
'Eurustheus slew the monsters, purged the world!'
So shall each poem pass you and imprint
Shame on the strange assurance. You praised Peace?
Sing him full-face, Kresphontes! 'Peace' the theme?
'Peace, in whom depths of wealth lie,—of the blest
Immortals beauteousest,—
Come! for the heart within me dies away,
So long dost thou delay!
Oh, I have feared lest old age, much annoy,
Conquer me, quite outstrip the tardy joy,
Thy gracious triumph-season I would see,
The song, the dance, the sport, profuse of crowns to be.
But come! for my sake, goddess great and dear.
Come to the city here!
Hateful Sedition drive thou from our homes,
With Her who madly roams
Rejoicing in the steel against the life
That 's whetted—banish Strife!'

"Shall I proceed? No need of next and next!
That were too easy, play so presses play,
Trooping tumultuous, each with instance apt,
Each eager to confute the idle boast!
What virtue but stands forth panegyrized,
What vice, unburned by stigma, in the books
Which bettered Hellas,—beyond graven gold
Or gem-indenture, sung by Phoibos' self
And saved in Kunthia's mountain treasure-house—
Ere you, man, moralist, were youth or boy?
—Not praise which, in the proffer, mocks the praised
By sly admixture of the blameworthy
And enforced coupling of base fellowship,—
Not blame which gloats the while it frowning laughs,
'Allow one glance on horrors—laughable!'—

This man's entire of heart and soul, discharged
Its love or hate, each unalloyed by each,
On objects worthy either; earnestness,
Attribute him, and power! but novelty?
Nor his nor yours a doctrine—all the world's!
What man of full-grown sense and sanity
Holds other than the truth,—wide Hellas through,—
Though truth he acts discredit truth he holds?
What imbecile has dared to formulate
'Love war, hate peace, become a litigant!'—
And so preach on, reverse each rule of right
Because he quarrels, combats, goes to law?
No, for his comment runs, with smile or sigh
According to heart's temper, 'Peace were best,
Except occasions when we put aside
Peace, and bid all the blessings in her gift
Quick join the crows, for sake of Marathon!'

"'Nay,' you reply; for one, whose mind withstands
His heart, and, loving peace, for conscience' sake
Wants war,—you find a crowd of hypocrites
Whose conscience means ambition, grudge and greed.
On such, reproof, sonorous doctrine, melts
Distilled like universal but thin dew
Which all too sparsely covers country: dear,
No doubt, to universal crop and clown,
Still, each bedewed keeps his own head-gear dry
With upthrust skiadeion, shakes adroit
The droppings to his neighbor. No! collect
All of the moisture, leave unhurt the heads
Which nowise need a washing, save and store
And dash the whole condensed to one fierce spout
On some one evil-doer, sheltered close,—
The fool supposed,—till you beat guard away,
And showed your audience, not that war was wrong,
But Lamachos absurd,—case, crests and all,—
Not that democracy was blind of choice,
But Kleon and Huperbolos were shams:
Not superstition vile, but Nikias crazed,—
The concrete for the abstract; that's the way!
What matters Choros crying 'Hence, impure!'
You cried 'Ariphrades does thus and thus!'
Now, earnestness seems never earnest more
Than when it dons for garb—indifference;
So, there's much laughing: but, compensative,
When frowning follows laughter, then indeed
Scout innuendo, sarcasm, irony!—
Wit's polished warfare glancing at first graze

From off hard headpiece, coarsely-coated brain
O' the commonalty—whom, unless you prick
To purpose, what avails that finer pates
Succumb to simple scratching? Those—not these—
'T is Multitude, which, moved, fines Lamachos,
Banishes Kleon and burns Sokrates,
House over head, or, better, poisons him.
Therefore in dealing with King Multitude,
Club-drub the callous numskulls! In and in
Beat this essential consequential fact
That here they have a hater of the three,
Who hates in word, phrase, nickname, epithet
And illustration, beyond doubt at all!
And similarly, would you win assent
To—Peace, suppose? You tickle the tough hide
With good plain pleasure her concomitant—
And, past mistake again, exhibit Peace—
Peace, vintager and festive, cheesecake-time,
Hare-slice-and-peasoup-season, household-joy;
Theoria's beautiful belongings match
Opora's lavish condescendings: brief,
Since here the people are to judge, you press
Such argument as people understand:
If with exaggeration—what care you?

"Have I misunderstood you in the main?
No! then must answer be, such argument,
Such policy, no matter what good love
Or hate it help, in practice proves absurd,
Useless and null: henceforward intercepts
Sober effective blow at what you blame,
And renders nugatory rightful praise
Of thing or person. The coarse brush has daubed—
What room for the finer limner's pencil-mark?
Blame? You curse, rather, till who blames must blush—
Lean to apology or praise, more like!
Does garment, simpered o'er as white, prove gray?
'Black, blacker than Acharnian charcoal, black
Beyond Kimmerian, Stugian blackness black,'
You bawl, till men sigh 'nearer snowiness!'
What follows? What one faint-rewarding fall
Of foe belabored ne'er so lustily?
Laugh Lamachos from out the people's heart?
He died, commanding, 'hero,' say yourself!
Gibe Nikias into privacy?—nay, shake
Kleon a little from his arrogance
By cutting him to shoe-sole-shreds? I think,
He ruled his life long, and, when time was ripe,

Died fighting for amusement,—good tough hide!
Sokrates still goes up and down the streets,
And Aristullos puts his speech in book,
When both should be abolished long ago.
Nay, wretchedest of rags, Ariphrades—
You have been fouling that redoubtable
Harp-player, twenty years, with what effect?
Still he strums on, strums ever cheerily,
And earns his wage,—'Who minds a joke?' men say.
No, friend! The statues stand—mud-stained at most—
Titan or pygmy: what achieves their fall
Will be, long after mud is flung and spent,
Some clear thin spirit-thrust of lightning—truth!

"Your praise, then—honey-smearing helps your friend,
More than blame's ordure-smirch hurts foe, perhaps?
Peace, now, misunderstood, ne'er prized enough,
You have interpreted to ignorance
Till ignorance opes eye, bat-blind before,
And for the first time knows Peace means the power
On maw of pancake, cheese-cake, barley-cake,
No stop nor stint to stuffing. While, in camp,
Who fights chews rancid tunny, onions raw,
Peace sits at cosy feast with lamp and fire,
Complaisant smooth-sleeked flute-girls giggling gay.
How thick and fast the snow falls, freezing War
Who shrugs, campaigns it, and may break a shin
Or twist an ankle! come, who hesitates
To give Peace, over War, the preference?
Ah, friend—had this indubitable fact
Haply occurred to poor Leonidas,
How had he turned tail on Thermopulai!
It cannot be that even his few wits
Were addled to the point that, so advised,
Preposterous he had answered—'Cakes are prime,
Hearth-sides are snug, sleek dancing-girls have worth,
And yet—for country's sake, to save our gods
Their temples, save our ancestors their tombs,
Save wife and child and home and liberty,—
I would chew sliced salt-fish, bear snow—nay, starve,
If need were,—and by much prefer the choice!'
Why, friend, your genuine hero, all the while,
Has been—who served precisely for your butt—
Kleonumos that, wise, cast shield away
On battle-ground; cried 'Cake my buckler be,
Embossed with cream-clot! peace, not war, I choose,
Holding with Dikaiopolis!' Comedy
Shall triumph, Dikaiopolis win assent,

When Miltiades shall next shirk Marathon,
Themistokles swap Salamis for—cake,
And Kimon grunt 'Peace, grant me dancing-girls!'
But sooner, hardly! twenty-five years since,
The war began,—such pleas for Peace have reached
A reasonable age. The end shows all!
And so with all the rest you advocate!
'Wise folk leave litigation! 'ware the wasps!
Whoso loves law and lawyers, heliast-like,
Wants hemlock!' None shows that so funnily.
But, once cure madness, how comports himself
Your sane exemplar, what 's our gain thereby?
Philokleon turns Bdelukleon! just this change,—
New sanity gets straightway drunk as sow,
Cheats baker-wives, brawls, kicks, cuffs, curses folk,
Parades a shameless flute-girl, bandies filth
With his own son who cured his father's cold
By making him catch fever—funnily!
But as for curing love of lawsuits—faugh!

"And how does new improve upon the old
—Your boast—in even abusing? Rough, may be—
Still, honest was the old mode. 'Call thief—thief!'
But never call thief even—murderer!
Much less call fop and fribble, worse one whit
Than fribble and fop! Spare neither! beat your brains
For adequate invective,—cut the life
Clean out each quality,—but load your lash
With no least lie, or we pluck scourge from hand!
Does poet want a whipping, write bad verse,
Inculcate foul deeds? There 's the fault to flog!
You vow, 'The rascal cannot read nor write,
Spends more in buying fish than Morsimos,
Somebody helps his Muse and courts his wife,
His uncle deals in crockery, and last—
Himself 's a stranger!' That 's the cap and crown
Of stinging-nettle, that 's the master-stroke!
What poet-rival,—after 'housebreaker,'
'Fish-gorging,' 'midnight footpad,' and so forth,—
Proves not, beside, 'a stranger'? Chased from charge
To charge, and, lie by lie, laughed out of court,—
Lo, wit's sure refuge, satire's grand resource—
All, from Kratinos downward—'strangers' they!
Pity the trick's too facile! None so raw
Among your playmates but have caught the ball
And sent it back as briskly to—yourself!
You too, my Attic, are styled 'stranger'—Rhodes,
Aigina, Lindos or Kameiros,—nay,

'T was Egypt reared (if Eupolis be right)
Who wrote the comedy (Kratinos vows)
Kratinos helped a little! Kleon's self
Was nigh promoted Comic, when he haled
My poet into court, and o'er the coals
Hauled and re-hauled 'the stranger,—insolent,
Who brought out plays, usurped our privilege!'
Why must you Comics one and all take stand
On lower ground than truth from first to last?
Why all agree to let folk disbelieve,
So laughter but reward a funny lie?
Repel such onslaughts—answer, sad and grave,
Your fancy-fleerings—who would stoop so low?
Your own adherents whisper,—when disgust
Too menacingly thrills Logeion through
At—Perikles invents this present war
Because men robbed his mistress of three maids—
Or—Sokrates wants burning, house o'er head,—
'What, so obtuse, not read between the lines?
Our poet means no mischief! All should know—
Ribaldry here implies a compliment!
He deals with things, not men,—his men are things—
Each represents a class, plays figure-head
And names the ship: no meaner than the first
Would serve; he styles a trireme "Sokrates"—
Fears "Sokrates" may prove unseaworthy,
(That's merely—"Sophists are the bane of boys")
Rat-riddled ("they are capable of theft")
Rotten or whatsoe'er shows ship-disease,
("They war with gods and worship whirligig.")
You never took the joke for earnest? scarce
Supposed mere figure-head meant entire ship,
And Sokrates—the whole fraternity?'

"This then is Comedy, our sacred song,
Censor of vice, and virtue's guard as sure:
Manners-instructing, morals' stop-estray,
Which, born a twin with public liberty,
Thrives with its welfare, dwindles with its wane!
Liberty? what so exquisitely framed
And fitted to suck dry its life of life
To last faint fibre?—since that life is truth.
You who profess your indignation swells
At sophistry, when specious words confuse
Deeds right and wrong, distinct before, you say—
(Though all that 's done is—dare veracity,
Show that the true conception of each deed
Affirmed, in vulgar parlance, 'wrong' or 'right,'

Proves to be neither, as the hasty hold,
But, change your side, shoots light, where dark alone
Was apprehended by the vulgar sense)—
You who put sophistry to shame, and shout
'There 's but a single side to man and thing;
A side so much more big than thing or man
Possibly can be, that—believe 't is true?
Such were too marvellous simplicity!'—
Confess, those sophists whom yourself depict,
(—Abide by your own painting!) what they teach,
They wish at least their pupil to believe,
And, what believe, to practise! Did you wish
Hellas should haste, as taught, with torch in hand,
And fire the horrid Speculation-shop?
Straight the shop's master rose and showed the mob
What man was your so monstrous Sokrates;
Himself received amusement, why not they?
Just as did Kleon first play magistrate
And bid you put your birth in evidence—
Since no unbadged buffoon is licensed here
To shame us all when foreign guests may mock—
Then,—birth established, fooling licensed you,—
He, duty done, resumed mere auditor,
Laughed with the loudest at his Lamia-shape,
Kukloboros-roaring, and the camel-rest.
Nay, Aristullos,—once your volley spent
On the male-Kirké and her swinish crew,—
PLATON,—so others call the youth we love,—
Sends your performance to the curious king—
'Do you desire to know Athenai's knack
At turning seriousness to pleasantry?
Read this! One Aristullos means myself.
The author is indeed a merry grig!'
Nay, it would seem as if yourself were bent
On laying down the law, 'Tell lies I must—
Aforethought and of purpose, no mistake!'
When forth yourself step, tell us from the stage,
'Here you behold the King of Comedy—
Me, who, the first, have purged my every piece
From each and all my predecessors' filth,
Abjured those satyr-adjuncts sewn to bid
The boys laugh, satyr-jokes whereof not one
Least sample but would make my hair turn gray
Beyond a twelvemonth's ravage! I renounce
Mountebank-claptrap, such as firework-fizz
And torchflare, or else nuts and barleycorns
Scattered among the crowd, to scramble for
And stop their mouths with; no such stuff shames me!

Who—what's more serious—know both when to strike
And when to stay my hand: once dead, my foe,
Why, done, my fighting! I attack a corpse?
I spare the corpse-like even! punish age?
I pity from my soul that sad effete
Toothless old mumbler called Kratinos! once
My rival,—now, alack, the dotard slinks
Ragged and hungry to what hole 's his home;
Ay, slinks through byways where no passenger
Flings him a bone to pick. You formerly
Adored the Muses' darling: dotard now,
Why, he may starve! O mob most mutable!'
So you harangued in person; while,—to point
Precisely out, these were but lies you launched,—
Prompt, a play followed primed with satyr-frisks,
No spice spared of the stomach-turning stew,
Full-fraught with torch-display, and barley-throw,
And Kleon, dead enough, bedaubed afresh;
While daft Kratinos—home to hole trudged he,
Wrung dry his wit to the last vinous dregs,
Decanted them to 'Bottle,'—beat, next year,—
'Bottle' and dregs—your best of 'Clouds' and dew!
Where, Comic King, may keenest eye detect
Improvement on your predecessors' work
Except in lying more audaciously?

"Why—genius! That's the grandeur, that 's the gold—
That 's you—superlatively true to touch—
Gold, leaf or lump—gold, anyhow the mass
Takes manufacture and proves Pallas' casque
Or, at your choice, simply a cask to keep
Corruption from decay. Your rivals' hoard
May ooze forth, lacking such preservative:
Yours cannot—gold plays guardian far too well!
Genius, I call you: dross, your rivals share;
Ay, share and share alike, too! says the world,
However you pretend supremacy
In aught beside that gold, your very own.
Satire? 'Kratinos for our satirist!'
The world cries. Elegance? 'Who elegant
As Eupolis?' resounds as noisily.
Artistic fancy? Choros-creatures quaint?
Magnes invented 'Birds' and 'Frogs' enough,
Archippos punned, Hegemon parodied,
To heart's content, before you stepped on stage.
Moral invective? Eupolis exposed
'That prating beggar, he who stole the cup,'
Before your 'Clouds' rained grime on Sokrates;

Nay, what beat 'Clouds' but 'Konnos,' muck for mud?
Courage? How long before, well-masked, you poured
Abuse on Eukrates and Lusikles,
Did Telekleides and Hermippos pelt
Their Perikles and Kumon? standing forth,
Bareheaded, not safe crouched behind a name,—
Philonides or else Kallistratos,
Put forth, when danger threatened,—mask for face,
To bear the brunt,—if blame fell, take the blame,—
If praise … why, frank laughed Aristophanes
'They write such rare stuff? No, I promise you!'
Rather, I see all true improvements, made
Or making, go against you—tooth and nail
Contended with; 't is still Moruchides,
'T is Euthumenes, Surakosios, nay,
Argurrhios and Kinesias,—common sense
And public shame, these only cleanse your sty!
Coerced, prohibited,—you grin and bear,
And, soon as may be, hug to heart again
The banished nastiness too dear to drop!
Krates could teach and practise festive song
Yet scorn scurrility; as gay and good,
Pherekrates could follow. Who loosed hold,
Must let fall rose-wreath, stoop to muck once more?
Did your particular self advance in aught,
Task the sad genius—steady slave the while—
To further—say, the patriotic aim?
No, there 's deterioration manifest
Year by year, play by play! survey them all,
From that boy's-triumph when 'Acharnes' dawned,
To 'Thesmophoriazousai,'—this man's-shame!
There, truly, patriot zeal so prominent
Allowed friends' plea perhaps: the baser stuff
Was but the nobler spirit's vehicle.
Who would imprison, unvolatilize
A violet's perfume, blends with fatty oils
Essence too fugitive in flower alone;
So, calling unguent—violet, call the play—
Obscenity impregnated with 'Peace'!
But here 's the boy grown bald, and here 's the play
With twenty years' experience: where 's one spice
Of odor in the hogs'-lard? what pretends
To aught except a grease-pot's quality?
Friend, sophist-hating! know,—worst sophistry
Is when man's own soul plays its own self false,
Reasons a vice into a virtue, pleads
'I detail sin to shame its author'—not
'I shame Ariphrades for sin's display!'

'I show Opora to commend Sweet Home'—
Not 'I show Bacchis for the striplings' sake!'

"Yet all the same—O genius and O gold—
Had genius ne'er diverted gold from use
Worthy the temple, to do copper's work
And coat a swine's trough—which abundantly
Might furnish Phoibos' tripod, Pallas' throne!
Had you, I dream, discarding all the base,
The brutish, spurned alone convention's watch
And ward against invading decency
Disguised as license, law in lawlessness,
And so, re-ordinating outworn rule,
Made Comedy and Tragedy combine,
Prove some new Both-yet-neither, all one bard,
Euripides with Aristophanes
Co-operant! this, reproducing Now
As that gave Then existence: Life to-day,
This, as that other—Life dead long ago!
The mob decrees such feat no crown, perchance,
But—why call crowning the reward of quest?
Tell him, my other poet,—where thou walk'st
Some rarer world than e'er Ilissos washed!

"But dream goes idly in the air. To earth!
Earth's question just amounts to—which succeeds,
Which fails of two life-long antagonists?
Suppose my charges all mistake! assume
Your end, despite ambiguous means, the best—
The only! you and he, a patriot-pair,
Have striven alike for one result—say, Peace!
You spoke your best straight to the arbiters—
Our people: have you made them end this war
By dint of laughter and abuse and lies
And postures of Opora? Sadly—No!
This war, despite your twenty-five years' work,
May yet endure until Athenai falls,
And freedom falls with her. So much for you!
Now, the antagonist Euripides—
Has he succeeded better? Who shall say?
He spoke quite o'er the heads of Kleon's crowd
To a dim future, and if there he fail,
Why, you are fellows in adversity.
But that 's unlike the fate of wise words launched
By music on their voyage. Hail, Depart,
Arrive, Glad Welcome! Not my single wish—
Yours also wafts the white sail on its way,
Your nature too is kingly. All beside

I call pretension,—no true potentate,
Whatever intermediary be crowned,
Zeus or Poseidon, where the vulgar sky
Lacks not Triballos to complete the group.
I recognize—behind such phantom-crew—
Necessity, Creation, Poet's Power,
Else never had I dared approach, appeal
To poetry, power, Aristophanes!
But I trust truth's inherent kingliness,
Trust who, by reason of much truth, shall reign
More or less royally—may prayer but push
His sway past limit, purge the false from true!
Nor, even so, had boldness nerved my tongue
But that the other king stands suddenly,
In all the grand investiture of death,
Bowing your knee beside my lowly head—
Equals one moment!

        "Now, arise and go!
Both have done homage to Euripides!"

Silence pursued the words: till he broke out—

"Scarce so! This constitutes, I may believe,
Sufficient homage done by who defames
Your poet's foe, since you account me such;
But homage-proper,—pay it by defence
Of him, direct defence and not oblique,
Not by mere mild admonishment of me!"

"Defence? The best, the only!" I replied.
"A story goes—When Sophokles, last year,
Cited before tribunal by his son
(A poet—to complete the parallel),
Was certified unsound of intellect,
And claimed as only fit for tutelage,
Since old and doting and incompetent
To carry on this world's work,—the defence
Consisted just in his reciting (calm
As the verse bore, which sets our heart a-swell
And voice a-heaving too tempestuously)
That choros-chant 'The station of the steed,
Stranger! thou comest to,—Kolonos white!'
Then he looked round and all revolt was dead.
You know the one adventure of my life—
What made Euripides Balaustion's friend.
When I last saw him, as he bade farewell,
'I sang another "Herakles,"' smiled he;

'It gained no prize: your love be prize I gain!
Take it—the tablets also where I traced
The story first with stulos pendent still—
Nay, the psalterion may complete the gift,
So, should you croon the ode bewailing Age,
Yourself shall modulate—same notes, same strings—
With the old friend who loved Balaustion once.'
There they lie! When you broke our solitude,
We were about to honor him once more
By reading the consummate Tragedy.
Night is advanced; I have small mind to sleep;
May I go on, and read,—so make defence,
So test true godship? You affirm, not I,
—Beating the god, affords such test: I hold
That when rash hands but touch divinity,
The chains drop off, the prison-walls dispart,
And—fire—he fronts mad Pentheus! Dare we try?"

Accordingly I read the perfect piece.

HERAKLES
Amphitruon. Zeus' Couchmate,—who of mortals knows not me,
Argive Amphitruon whom Alkaios sired
Of old, as Perseus him, I—Herakles?
My home, this Thebai where the earth-born spike
Of Sown-ones burgeoned: Ares saved from these
A handful of their seed that stocks to-day
With children's children Thebai, Kadmos built.
Of these had Kreon birth, Menoikeus' child,
King of the country,—Kreon that became
The father of this woman, Megara,
Whom, when time was, Kadmeians one and all
Pealed praise to, marriage-songs with fluted help,
While to my dwelling that grand Herakles
Bore her, his bride. But, leaving Thebes—where I
Abode perforce—this Megara and those
Her kinsmen, the desire possessed my son
Rather to dwell in Argos, that walled work,
Kuklopian city, which I fly, myself,
Because I slew Elektruon. Seeking so
To ease away my hardships and once more
Inhabit his own land, for my return
Heavy the price he pays Eurustheus there—
The letting in of light on this choked world!
Either he promised, vanquished by the goad
Of Heré, or because fate willed it thus.
The other labors—why, he toiled them through;

But for this last one—down by Tainaros,
Its mouth, to Haides' realm descended he
To drag into the light the three-shaped hound
Of Hell: whence Herakles returns no more.
Now, there 's an old-world tale, Kadmeians have,
How Dirké's husband was a Lukos once,
Holding the seven-towered city here in sway
Before they ruled the land, white-steeded pair,
The twins Amphion, Zethos, born to Zeus.
This Lukos' son,—named like his father too,
No born Kadmeian but Euboia's gift,—
Comes and kills Kreon, lords it o'er the land,
Falling upon our town sedition-sick.
To us, akin to Kreon, just that bond
Becomes the worst of evils, seemingly;
For, since my son in the earth's abysms,
This man of valor, Lukos, lord and king,
Seeks now to slay these sons of Herakles,
And slay his wife as well,—by murder thus
Thinking to stamp out murder,—slay too me,
(If me 't is fit you count among men still,—
Useless old age,) and all for fear lest these,
Grown men one day, exact due punishment
Of bloodshed and their mother's father's fate.
I therefore, since he leaves me in these domes,
The children's household guardian,—left, when earth's
Dark dread he underwent, that son of mine,—
I, with their mother, lest his boys should die,
Sit at this altar of the savior Zeus
Which, glory of triumphant spear, he raised
Conquering—my nobly-born!—the Minuai.
Here do we guard our station, destitute
Of all things, drink, food, raiment, on bare ground
Couched side by side: sealed out of house and home
Sit we in a resourcelessness of help.
Our friends—why, some are no true friends, I see!
The rest, that are true, want the means to aid.
So operates in man adversity:
Whereof may never anybody—no,
Though half of him should really wish me well,—
Happen to taste! a friend-test faultless, that!

MEGARA
Old man, who erst did raze the Taphian town,
Illustriously, the army-leader, thou,
Of speared Kadmeians—how gods play men false!
I, now, missed nowise fortune in my sire,
Who, for his wealth, was boasted mighty once,

Having supreme rule,—for the love of which
Leap the long lances forth at favored breasts,—
And having children too: and me he gave
Thy son, his house with that of Herakles
Uniting by the far-famed marriage-bed.
And now these things are dead and flown away.
While thou and I await our death, old man,
These Herakleian boys too, whom—my chicks—
I save beneath my wings like brooding bird.
But one or other falls to questioning.
"O mother," cries he, "where in all the world
Is father gone to? What 's he doing? when
Will he come back?" At fault through tender years,
They seek their sire. For me, I put them off,
Telling them stories; at each creak of doors,
All wonder "Does he come?"—and all a-foot
Make for the fall before the parent knee.
Now then, what hope, what method of escape
Facilitatest thou?—for, thee, old man,
I look to,—since we may not leave by stealth
The limits of the land, and guards, more strong
Than we, are at the outlets: nor in friends
Remain to us the hopes of safety more.
Therefore, whatever thy decision be,
Impart it for the common good of all!
Lest now should prove the proper time to die,
Though, being weak, we spin it out and live.

AMPHITRUON
Daughter, it scarce is easy, do one's best,
To blurt out counsel, things at such a pass.

MEGARA
You want some sorrow more, or so love life?

AMPHITRUON
I both enjoy life, and love hopes beside.

MEGARA
And I; but hope against hope—no, old man!

AMPHITRUON
In these delayings of an ill lurks cure.

MEGARA
But bitter is the meantime, and it bites.

AMPHITRUON

Oh, there may be a run before the wind
From out these present ills, for me and thee,
Daughter, and yet may come my son, thy spouse!
But hush! and from the children take away
Their founts aflow with tears, and talk them calm,
Steal them by stories—sad theft, all the same!
For, human troubles—they grow weary too;
Neither the wind-blasts always have their strength,
Nor happy men keep happy to the end:
Since all things change—their natures part in twain;
And that man's bravest therefore, who hopes on,
Hopes ever: to despair is coward-like.

CHOROS
These domes that overroof,
This long-used couch, I come to, having made
A staff my prop, that song may put to proof
The swan-like power, age-whitened,—poet's aid
Of sobbed-forth dirges—words that stand aloof
From action now: such am I—just a shade
With night for all its face, a mere night-dream—
And words that tremble too: howe'er they seem,
Devoted words, I deem.

O of a father ye unfathered ones,
O thou old man, and thou whose groaning stuns—
Unhappy mother—only us above,
Nor reaches him below in Haides' realm, thy love!
—(Faint not too soon, urge forward foot and limb
Way-weary, nor lose courage—as some horse
Yoked to the car whose weight recoils on him
Just at the rock-ridge that concludes his course!
Take by the hand, the peplos, any one
Whose foothold fails him, printless and fordone!
Aged, assist along me aged too,
Who,—mate with thee in toils when life was new,
And shields and spears first made acquaintanceship,—
Stood by thyself and proved no bastard-slip
Of fatherland when loftiest glory grew.)—
See now, how like the sire's
Each eyeball fiercely fires!
What though ill-fortune have not left his race?
Neither is gone the grand paternal grace!
Hellas! O what—what combatants, destroyed
In these, wilt thou one day seek—seek, and find all void!

Pause! for I see the ruler of this land,
Lukos, now passing through the palace-gate.

LUKOS

The Herakleian couple—father, wife—
If needs I must, I question: "must" forsooth?
Being your master—all I please, I ask.
To what time do you seek to spin out life?
What hope, what help see, so as not to die?
Is it you trust the sire of these, that 's sunk
In Haides, will return? How past the pitch,
Suppose you have to die, you pile the woe—
Thou, casting, Hellas through, thy empty vaunts
As though Zeus helped thee to a god for son;
And thou, that thou wast styled our best man's wife!
Where was the awful in his work wound up,
If he did quell and quench the marshy snake
Or the Nemeian monster whom he snared
And—says, by throttlings of his arm, he slew?
With these do you outwrestle me? Such feats
Shall save from death the sons of Herakles
Who got praise, being naught, for bravery
In wild-beast-battle, otherwise a blank?
No man to throw on left arm buckler's weight,
Not he, nor get in spear's reach! bow he bore—
True coward's-weapon: shoot first and then fly!
No bow-and-arrow proves a man is brave,
But who keeps rank,—stands, one unwinking stare
As, ploughing up, the darts come,—brave is he.
My action has no impudence, old man!
Providence, rather: for I own I slew
Kreon, this woman's sire, and have his seat.
Nowise I wish, then, to leave, these grown up,
Avengers on me, payment for my deeds.

AMPHITRUON

As to the part of Zeus in his own child,
Let Zeus defend that! As to mine, 't is me
The care concerns to show by argument
The folly of this fellow,—Herakles,
Whom I stand up for! since to hear thee styled—
Cowardly—that is unendurable.
First then, the infamous (for I account
Amongst the words denied to human speech,
Timidity ascribed thee, Herakles!)
This I must put from thee, with gods in proof.
Zeus' thunder I appeal to, those four steeds
Whereof he also was the charioteer
When, having shut down the earth's Giant-growth—
(Never shaft flew but found and fitted flank)—

Triumph he sang in common with the gods.
The Kentaur-race, four-footed insolence—
Go ask at Pholoé, vilest thou of kings,
Whom they would pick out and pronounce best man,
If not my son, "the seeming-brave," say'st thou!
But Dirphus, thy Abantid mother-town,
Question her, and she would not praise, I think!
For there 's no spot, where having done some good,
Thy country thou might'st call to witness worth.
Now, that allwise invention, archer's-gear,
Thou blamest: hear my teaching and grow sage!
A man in armor is his armor's slave,
And, mixed with rank and file that want to run,
He dies because his neighbors have lost heart.
Then, should he break his spear, no way remains
Of warding death off,—gone that body-guard,
His one and only; while, whatever folk
Have the true bow-hand,—here 's the one main good,—
Though he have sent ten thousand shafts abroad,
Others remain wherewith the archer saves
His limbs and life, too,—stands afar and wards
Away from flesh the foe that vainly stares
Hurt by the viewless arrow, while himself
Offers no full front to those opposite,
But keeps in thorough cover: there 's the point
That 's capital in combat—damage foe,
Yet keep a safe skin—foe not out of reach
As you are! Thus my words contrast with thine,
And such, in judging facts, our difference.
These children, now, why dost thou seek to slay?
What have they done thee? In a single point
I count thee wise—if, being base thyself,
Thou dread'st the progeny of nobleness.
Yet this bears hard upon us, all the same,
If we must die—because of fear in thee—
A death 't were fit thou suffer at our hands,
Thy betters, did Zeus rightly judge us all.
If therefore thou art bent on sceptre-sway,
Thyself, here—suffer us to leave the land,
Fugitives! nothing do by violence,
Or violence thyself shalt undergo
When the gods' gale may chance to change for thee!
Alas, O land of Kadmos,—for 't is thee
I mean to close with, dealing out the due
Revilement,—in such sort dost thou defend
Herakles and his children? Herakles
Who, coming, one to all the world, against
The Minuai, fought them and left Thebes an eye

Unblinded henceforth to front freedom with!
Neither do I praise Hellas, nor shall brook
Ever to keep in silence that I count
Towards my son, craven of cravens—her
Whom it behooved go bring the young ones here
Fire, spears, arms—in exchange for seas made safe,
And cleansings of the land, his labor's price.
But fire, spears, arms,—O children, neither Thebes
Nor Hellas has them for you! 'T is myself,
A feeble friend, ye look to: nothing now
But a tongue's murmur, for the strength is gone
We had once, and with age are limbs a-shake
And force a-flicker! Were I only young,
Still with the mastery o'er bone and thew,
Grasping first spear that came, the yellow locks
Of this insulter would I bloody so—
Should send him skipping o'er the Atlantic bounds
Out of my arm's reach through poltroonery!

CHOROS
Have not the really good folk starting-points
For speech to purpose,—though rare talkers they?

LUKOS
Say thou against us words thou towerest with!
I, for thy words, will deal thee blows, their due.
Go, some to Helikon, to Parnasos
Some, and the clefts there! Bid the woodmen fell
Oak-trunks, and, when the same are brought inside
The city, pile the altar round with logs,
Then fire it, burn the bodies of them all,
That they may learn thereby, no dead man rules
The land here, but 't is I, by acts like these!
As for you, old sirs, who are set against
My judgments, you shall groan for—not alone
The Herakleian children, but the fate
Of your own house beside, when faring ill
By any chance: and you shall recollect
Slaves are you of a tyranny that 's mine!

CHOROS
O progeny of earth,—whom Ares sowed
When he laid waste the dragon's greedy jaw—
Will ye not lift the staves, right-hand supports,
And bloody this man's irreligious head?
Who, being no Kadmeian, rules,—the wretch,—
Our easy youth: an interloper too!
But not of me, at least, shalt thou enjoy

Thy lordship ever; nor my labor's fruit—
Hand worked so hard for—have! A curse with thee,
Whence thou didst come, there go and tyrannize!
For never while I live shalt thou destroy
The Herakleian children: not so deep
Hides he below ground, leaving thee their lord!
But we bear both of you in mind,—that thou,
The land's destroyer, dost possess the land,
While he who saved it, loses every right.
I play the busybody—for I serve
My dead friends when they need friends' service most?
O right-hand, how thou yearnest to snatch spear
And serve indeed! in weakness dies the wish,
Or I had stayed thee calling me a slave,
And nobly drawn my breath at home in Thebes
Where thou exultest!—city that's insane,
Sick through sedition and bad government,
Else never had she gained for master—thee!

MEGARA
Old friends, I praise you: since a righteous wrath
For friend's sake well becomes a friend. But no!
On our account in anger with your lord,
Suffer no injury! Hear my advice,
Amphitruon, if I seem to speak aright.
Oh, yes, I love my children! how not love
What I brought forth, what toiled for? and to die—
Sad I esteem too; still, the fated way
Who stiffens him against, that man I count
Poor creature; us, who are of other mood,
Since we must die, behooves us meet our death
Not burnt to cinders, giving foes the laugh—
To me, worse ill than dying, that! we owe
Our houses many a brave deed, now to pay.
Thee, indeed, gloriously men estimate
For spear-work, so that unendurable
Were it that thou shouldst die a death of shame.
And for my glorious husband, where wants he
A witness that he would not save his boys
If touched in their good fame thereby? since birth
Bears ill with baseness done for children's sake,
My husband needs must be my pattern here.
See now thy hope—how much I count thereon!
Thou thinkest that thy son will come to light:
And, of the dead, who came from Haides back?
But we with talk this man might mollify:
Never! Of all foes, fly the foolish one!
Wise, well-bred people, make concession to!

Sooner you meet respect by speaking soft.
Already it was in my mind—perchance
We might beg off these children's banishment;
But even that is sad, involving them
In safety, ay—and piteous poverty!
Since the host's visage for the flying friend
Has, only one day, the sweet look, 'tis said.
Dare with us death, which waits thee, dared or no!
We call on thine ancestral worth, old man!
For who out-labors what the gods appoint
Shows energy, but energy gone mad.
Since what must—none e'er makes what must not be!

CHOROS

Had any one, while yet my arms were strong,
Been scorning thee, he easily had ceased.
But we are naught, now; thine henceforth to see—
Amphitruon, how to push aside these fates!

AMPHITRUON

Nor cowardice nor a desire of life
Stops me from dying: but I seek to save
My son his children. Vain! I set my heart,
It seems, upon impossibility.
See, it is ready for the sword, this throat
To pierce, divide, dash down from precipice!
But one grace grant us, king, we supplicate!
Slay me and this unhappy one before
The children, lest we see them—impious sight!—
Gasping the soul forth, calling all the while
On mother and on father's father! Else,
Do as thy heart inclines thee! No resource
Have we from death, and we resign ourselves.

MEGARA

And I too supplicate: add grace to grace,
And, though but one man, doubly serve us both!
Let me bestow adornment of the dead
Upon these children! Throw the palace wide!
For now we are shut out. Thence these shall share
At least so much of wealth was once their sire's!

LUKOS

These things shall be. Withdraw the bolts, I bid
My servants! Enter and adorn yourselves!
I grudge no peploi; but when these ye wind
About your bodies,—that adornment done,—
Then I shall come and give you to the grave.

MEGARA

O children, follow this unhappy foot,
Your mother's, into your ancestral home,
Where others have the power, are lords in truth,
Although the empty name is left us yet!

AMPHITRUON

O Zeus, in vain I had thee marriage-mate,
In vain I called thee father of my child!
Thou wast less friendly far than thou didst seem.
I, the mere man, o'ermatch in virtue thee
The mighty god: for I have not betrayed
The Herakleian children,—whereas thou
Hadst wit enough to come clandestinely
Into the chamber, take what no man gave,
Another's place; and when it comes to help
Thy loved ones, there thou lackest wit indeed!
Thou art some stupid god or born unjust.

CHOROS

Even a dirge, can Phoibos suit
In song to music jubilant
For all its sorrow: making shoot
His golden plectron o'er the lute,
Melodious ministrant.
And I, too, am of mind to raise,
Despite the imminence of doom,
A song of joy, outpour my praise
To him—what is it rumor says?—
Whether—now buried in the ghostly gloom
Below ground—he was child of Zeus indeed,
Or mere Amphitruon's mortal seed—
To him I weave the wreath of song, his labor's meed.
For, is my hero perished in the feat?
The virtues of brave toils, in death complete,
These save the dead in song,—their glory-garland meet!

First, then, he made the wood
Of Zeus a solitude,
Slaying its lion-tenant; and he spread
The tawniness behind—his yellow head
Enmuffled by the brute's, backed by that grin of dread.
The mountain-roving savage Kentaur-race
He strewed with deadly bow about their place,
Slaying with wingèd shafts: Peneios knew,
Beauteously-eddying, and the long tracts too
Of pasture trampled fruitless, and as well

Those desolated haunts Mount Pelion under,
And, grassy up to Homolé, each dell
Whence, having filled their hands with pine-tree plunder,
Horse-like was wont to prance from, and subdue
The land of Thessaly, that bestial crew.
The golden-headed spot-back'd stag he slew,
That robber of the rustics: glorified
Therewith the goddess who in hunter's pride
Slaughters the game along Oinoé's side.
And, yoked abreast, he brought the chariot-breed
To pace submissive to the bit, each steed
That in the bloody cribs of Diomede
Champed and, unbridled, hurried down that gore
For grain, exultant the dread feast before—
Of man's flesh: hideous feeders they of yore!
All as he crossed the Hebros' silver-flow
Accomplished he such labor, toiling so
For Mukenaian tyrant; ay, and more—
He crossed the Melian shore
And, by the sources of Amauros, shot
To death that strangers'-pest
Kuknos, who dwelt in Amphanaia: not
Of fame for good to guest!

And next, to the melodious maids he came,
Inside the Hesperian court-yard: hand must aim
At plucking gold fruit from the appled leaves,
Now he had killed the dragon, backed like flame,
Who guards the unapproachable he weaves
Himself all round, one spire about the same.
And into those sea-troughs of ocean dived
The hero, and for mortals calm contrived,
Whatever oars should follow in his wake.
And under heaven's mid-seat his hands thrust he,
At home with Atlas: and, for valor's sake,
Held the gods up their star-faced mansionry.
Also, the rider-host of Amazons
About Maiotis many-streamed, he went
To conquer through the billowy Euxin once,
Having collected what an armament
Of friends from Hellas, all on conquest bent
Of that gold-garnished cloak, dread girdle-chase!
So Hellas gained the girl's barbarian grace
And at Mukenai saves the trophy still—
Go wonder there, who will!

And the ten-thousand-headed hound
Of many a murder, the Lernaian snake

He burned out, head by head, and cast around
His darts a poison thence,—darts soon to slake
Their rage in that three-bodied herdsman's gore
Of Erutheia. Many a running more
He made for triumph and felicity,
And, last of toils, to Haides, never dry
Of tears, he sailed: and there he, luckless, ends
His life completely, nor returns again.
The house and home are desolate of friends,
And where the children's life-path leads them, plain
I see,—no step retraceable, no god
Availing, and no law to help the lost!
The oar of Charon marks their period,
Waits to end all. Thy hands, these roofs accost!—
To thee, though absent, look their uttermost!

But if in youth and strength I flourished still,
Still shook the spear in fight, did power match will
In these Kadmeian co-mates of my age,
They would,—and I,—when warfare was to wage,
Stand by these children; but I am bereft
Of youth now, lone of that good genius left!

But hist, desist! for here come these,—
Draped as the dead go, under and over,—
Children long since—now hard to discover—
Of the once so potent Herakles!
And the loved wife dragging, in one tether
About her feet, the boys together;
And the hero's aged sire comes last!
Unhappy that I am! Of tears which rise,—
How am I all unable to hold fast,
Longer, the aged fountains of these eyes!

MEGARA
Be it so! Who is priest, who butcher here
Of these ill-fated ones, or stops the breath
Of me, the miserable? Ready, see,
The sacrifice—to lead where Haides lives!
O children, we are led—no lovely team
Of corpses—age, youth, motherhood, all mixed!
O sad fate of myself and these my sons
Whom with these eyes I look at, this last time!
I, indeed, bore you: but for enemies
I brought you up to be a laughing-stock,
Matter for merriment, destruction-stuff!
Woe's me!
Strangely indeed my hopes have struck me down

From what I used to hope about you once—
The expectation from your father's talk!
For thee, now, thy dead sire dealt Argos to:
Thou wast to have Eurustheus' house one day,
And rule Pelasgia where the fine fruits grow;
And, for a stole of state, he wrapped about
Thy head with that the lion-monster bore,
That which himself went wearing armor-wise.
And thou wast King of Thebes—such chariots there!
Those plains I had for portion—all for thee,
As thou hadst coaxed them out of who gave birth
To thee, his boy: and into thy right hand
He thrust the guardian-club of Daidalos,—
Poor guardian proves the gift that plays thee false!
And upon thee he promised to bestow
Oichalia—what, with those far-shooting shafts,
He ravaged once; and so, since three you were,
With threefold kingdoms did he build you up
To very towers, your father,—proud enough,
Prognosticating, from your manliness
In boyhood, what the manhood's self would be.
For my part, I was picking out for you
Brides, suiting each with his alliance—this
From Athens, this from Sparté, this from Thebes—
Whence, suited—as stern-cables steady ship—
You might have hold on life gods bless. All gone!
Fortune turns round and gives us—you, the Fates
Instead of brides—me, tears for nuptial baths,
Unhappy in my hoping! And the sire
Of your sire—he prepares the marriage-feast
Befitting Haides who plays father now—
Bitter relationship! Oh me! which first—
Which last of you shall I to bosom fold?
To whom shall I fit close, his mouth to mine?
Of whom shall I lay hold and ne'er let go?
How would I gather, like the brown-winged bee,
The groans from all, and, gathered into one,
Give them you back again, a crowded tear!
Dearest, if any voice be heard of men
Dungeoned in Haides, thee—to thee I speak!
Here is thy father dying, and thy boys!
And I too perish, famed as fortunate
By mortals once, through thee! Assist them! Come!
But come! though just a shade, appear to me!
For, coming, thy ghost-grandeur would suffice,
Such cowards are they in thy presence, these
Who kill thy children now thy back is turned!

AMPHITRUON

Ay, daughter, bid the powers below assist!
But I will rather, raising hand to heaven,
Call thee to help, O Zeus, if thy intent
Be, to these children, helpful anyway,
Since soon thou wilt be valueless enough!
And yet thou hast been called and called; in vain
I labor: for we needs must die, it seems.
Well, aged brothers—life's a little thing!
Such as it is, then, pass life pleasantly
From day to night, nor once grieve all the while!
Since Time concerns him not about our hopes,—
To save them,—but his own work done, flies off.
Witness myself, looked up to among men,
Doing noteworthy deeds: when here comes fate
Lifts me away, like feather skyward borne,
In one day! Riches then and glory,—whom
These are found constant to, I know not. Friends,
Farewell! the man who loved you all so much,
Now, this last time, my mates, ye look upon!

MEGARA

Ha!
O father, do I see my dearest? Speak!

AMPHITRUON

No more than thou canst, daughter—dumb like thee!

MEGARA

Is this he whom we heard was under ground?

AMPHITRUON

Unless at least some dream in day we see!

MEGARA

What do I say? what dreams insanely view?
This is no other than thy son, old sire!
Here, children! hang to these paternal robes,
Quick, haste, hold hard on him, since here's your true
Zeus that can save—and every whit as well!

HERAKLES

Oh, hail, my palace, my hearth's propula,—
How glad I see thee as I come to light!
Ha, what means this? My children I behold
Before the house in garments of the grave,
Chapleted, and, amid a crowd of men,
My very wife—my father weeping too,

Whatever the misfortune! Come, best take
My station nearer these and learn it all!
Wife, what new sorrow has approached our home?

MEGARA

O dearest! light flashed on thy father now!
Art thou come? art thou saved and dost thou fall
On friends in their supreme extremity?

HERAKLES

How say'st thou? Father! what's the trouble here?

MEGARA

Undone are we!—but thou, old man, forgive
If first I snatch what thou shouldst say to him!
For somehow womanhood wakes pity more.
Here are my children killed and I undone!

HERAKLES

Apollon, with what preludes speech begins!

MEGARA

Dead are my brothers and old father too.

HERAKLES

How say'st thou?—doing what?—by spear-stroke whence?

MEGARA

Lukos destroyed them—the land's noble king!

HERAKLES

Met them in arms? or through the land's disease?

MEGARA

Sedition: and he sways seven-gated Thebes.

HERAKLES

Why then came fear on the old man and thee?

MEGARA

He meant to kill thy father, me, our boys.

HERAKLES

How say'st thou? Fearing what from orphanage?

MEGARA

Lest they should some day pay back Kreon's death.

HERAKLES
And why trick out the boys corpse-fashion thus?

MEGARA
These wraps of death we have already donned.

HERAKLES
And you had died through violence? Woe's me!

MEGARA
Left bare of friends: and thou wast dead, we heard.

HERAKLES
And whence came on you this faintheartedness?

MEGARA
The heralds of Eurustheus brought the news.

HERAKLES
And why was it you left my house and hearth?

MEGARA
Forced thence: thy father—from his very couch!

HERAKLES
And no shame at insulting the old man?

MEGARA
Shame, truly! no near neighbors he and Shame!

HERAKLES
And so much, in my absence, lacked I friends?

MEGARA
Friends,—are there any to a luckless man?

HERAKLES
The Minuai-war I waged,—they spat forth these?

MEGARA
Friendless—again I tell thee—is ill-luck.

HERAKLES
Will not you cast these hell-wraps from your hair
And look on light again, and with your eyes
Taste the sweet change from nether dark to day?
While I—for now there needs my handiwork—
First I shall go, demolish the abodes

Of these new lordships; next hew off the head
Accurst and toss it for the dogs to trail.
Then, such of the Kadmeians as I find
Were craven though they owed me gratitude,—
Some I intend to handle with this club
Renowned for conquest; and with wingèd shafts
Scatter the others, fill Ismenos full
With bloody corpses,—Dirké's flow so white
Shall be incarnadined. For, whom, I pray,
Behooves me rather help than wife and child
And aged father? Farewell, "Labors" mine!
Vainly I wrought them: my true work lay here!
My business is to die defending these,—
If for their father's sake they meant to die.
Or how shall we call brave the battling it
With snake and lion, as Eurustheus bade,
If yet I must not labor death away
From my own children? "Conquering Herakles"
Folk will not call me as they used, I think!
The right thing is for parents to assist
Children, old age, the partner of the couch.

AMPHITRUON

True, son! thy duty is—be friend to friends
And foe to foes: yet—no more haste than needs!

HERAKLES

Why, father, what is over-hasty here?

AMPHITRUON

Many a pauper—seeming to be rich,
As the word goes—the king calls partisan.
Such made a riot, ruined Thebes to rob
Their neighbor: for, what good they had at home
Was spent and gone,—flew off through idleness.
You came to trouble Thebes, they saw: since seen,
Beware lest, raising foes, a multitude,
You stumble where you apprehend no harm.

HERAKLES

If all Thebes saw me, not a whit care I.
But seeing as I did a certain bird
Not in the lucky seats, I knew some woe
Was fallen upon the house: so, purposely,
By stealth I made my way into the land.

AMPHITRUON

And now, advancing, hail the hearth with praise

And give the ancestral home thine eye to see!
For he himself will come, thy wife and sons
The drag-forth—slaughter—slay me too,—this king!
But, here remaining, all succeeds with thee—
Gain lost by no false step. So, this thy town
Disturb not, son, ere thou right matters here!

HERAKLES
Thus will I do, for thou say'st well; my home
Let me first enter! Since at the due time
Returning from the unsunned depths where dwells
Haides' wife Koré, let me not affront
Those gods beneath my roof, I first should hail!

AMPHITRUON
For didst thou really visit Haides, son?

HERAKLES
Ay—dragged to light, too, his three-headed beast.

AMPHITRUON
By fight didst conquer—or through Koré's gift?

HERAKLES
Fight: well for me, I saw the Orgies first!

AMPHITRUON
And is he in Eurustheus' house, the brute?

HERAKLES
Chthonia's grove, Hermion's city, holds him now.

AMPHITRUON
Does not Eurustheus know thee back on earth?

HERAKLES
No: I would come first and see matters here.

AMPHITRUON
But how wast thou below ground such a time?

HERAKLES
I stopped, from Haides, bringing Theseus up.

AMPHITRUON
And where is he?—bound o'er the plain for home?

HERAKLES

Gone glad to Athens—Haides' fugitive!
But, up, boys! follow father into house!
There's a far better going-in for you
Truly, than going-out was! Nay, take heart,
And let the eyes no longer run and run!
And thou, O wife, my own, collect thy soul
Nor tremble now! Leave grasping, all of you,
My garments! I'm not winged, nor fly from friends!
Ah,—
No letting go for these, who all the more
Hang to my garments! Did you foot indeed
The razor's edge? Why, then I'll carry them—
Take with my hands these small craft up, and tow
Just as a ship would. There! don't fear I shirk
My children's service! this way, men are men,
No difference! best and worst, they love their boys
After one fashion: wealth they differ in—
Some have it, others not; but each and all
Combine to form the children-loving race.

CHOROS
Youth is a pleasant burden to me;
But age on my head, more heavily
Than the crags of Aitna, weighs and weighs,
And darkening cloaks the lids and intercepts the rays.
Never be mine the preference
Of an Asian empire's wealth, nor yet
Of a house all gold, to youth, to youth
That's beauty, whatever the gods dispense!
Whether in wealth we joy, or fret
Paupers,—of all God's gifts most beautiful, in truth!

But miserable murderous age I hate!
Let it go to wreck, the waves adown,
Nor ever by rights plague tower or town
Where mortals bide, but still elate
With wings, on ether, precipitate,
Wander them round—nor wait!

But if the gods, to man's degree,
Had wit and wisdom, they would bring
Mankind a twofold youth, to be
Their virtue's sign-mark, all should see,
In those with whom life's winter thus grew spring.
For when they died, into the sun once more
Would they have traversed twice life's race-course o'er;
While ignobility had simply run
Existence through, nor second life begun,

And so might we discern both bad and good
As surely as the starry multitude
Is numbered by the sailors, one and one.
But now the gods by no apparent line
Limit the worthy and the base define;
Only, a certain period rounds, and so
Brings man more wealth,—but youthful vigor, no!

Well! I am not to pause
Mingling together—wine and wine in cup—
The Graces with the Muses up—
Most dulcet marriage: loosed from music's laws,
No life for me!
But where the wreaths abound, there ever may I be!
And still, an aged bard, I shout Mnemosuné—
Still chant of Herakles the triumph-chant,
Companioned by the seven-stringed tortoise-shell
And Libuan flute, and Bromios' self as well,
God of the grape, with man participant!
Not yet will we arrest their glad advance—
The Muses who so long have led me forth to dance!
A paian—hymn the Delian girls indeed,
Weaving a beauteous measure in and out
His temple-gates, Latona's goodly seed;
And paians—I too, these thy domes about,
From these gray cheeks, my king, will swan-like shout—
Old songster! Ay, in song it starts off brave—
"Zeus' son is he!" and yet, such grace of birth
Surpassing far, to man his labors gave
Existence, one calm flow without a wave,
Having destroyed the beasts, the terrors of the earth.

LUKOS
From out the house Amphitruon comes—in time!
For 'tis a long while now since ye bedecked
Your bodies with the dead-folks' finery.
But quick! the boys and wife of Herakles—
Bid them appear outside this house, keep pact
To die, and need no bidding but your own!

AMPHITRUON
King! you press hard on me sore-pressed enough,
And give me scorn—beside my dead ones here.
Meet in such matters were it, though you reign,
To temper zeal with moderation. Since
You do impose on us the need to die—
Needs must we love our lot, obey your will.

LUKOS

Where's Megara, then? Alkmené's grandsons, where?

AMPHITRUON

She, I think,—as one figures from outside,—

LUKOS

Well, this same thinking,—what affords its ground?

AMPHITRUON

—Sits suppliant on the holy altar-steps,—

LUKOS

Idly indeed a suppliant to save life!

AMPHITRUON

—And calls on her dead husband, vainly too!

LUKOS

For he's not come, nor ever will arrive.

AMPHITRUON

Never—at least, if no god raise him up.

LUKOS

Go to her, and conduct her from the house!

AMPHITRUON

I should partake the murder, doing that.

LUKOS

We,—since thou hast a scruple in the case,—
Outside of fears, we shall march forth these lads,
Mother and all. Here, follow me, my folk—
And gladly so remove what stops our toils!

AMPHITRUON

Thou—go then! March where needs must! What remains—
Perhaps concerns another. Doing ill,
Expect some ill be done thee!
Ha, old friends!
On he strides beautifully! in the toils
O' the net, where swords spring forth, will he be fast—
Minded to kill his neighbors—the arch-knave!
I go, too—I must see the falling corpse!
For he has sweets to give—a dying man,
Your foe, that pays the price of deeds he did.

CHOROS

Troubles are over! He the great king once,
Turns the point, tends for Haides, goal of life!
O justice, and the gods' back-flowing fate!

AMPHITRUON

Thou art come, late indeed, where death pays crime—
These insults heaped on better than thyself!

CHOROS

Joy gives this outburst to my tears! Again
Come round those deeds, his doing, which of old
He never dreamed himself was to endure—
King of the country! But enough, old man!
Indoors, now, let us see how matters stand—
If somebody be faring as I wish!

LUKOS

Ah me—me!

CHOROS

This strikes the keynote—music to my mind,
Merry i' the household! Death takes up the tune!
The king gives voice, groans murder's prelude well!

LUKOS

O all the land of Kadmos! slain by guile!

CHOROS

Ay, for who slew first? Paying back thy due,
Resign thee! make, for deeds done, mere amends!
Who was it grazed the gods through lawlessness—
Mortal himself, threw up his fools'-conceit
Against the blessed heavenly ones—as though
Gods had no power? Old friends, the impious man
Exists not any more! The house is mute.
Turn we to song and dance! For, those I love,
Those I wish well to, well fare they, to wish!

Dances, dances and banqueting
To Thebes, the sacred city through,
Are a care! for, change and change
Of tears to laughter, old to new,
Our lays, glad birth, they bring, they bring!
He is gone and past, the mighty king!
And the old one reigns, returned—Oh, strange!
From the Acherontian harbor too!
Advent of hope, beyond thought's widest range!

To the gods, the gods, are crimes a care,
And they watch our virtue, well aware
That gold and that prosperity drive man
Out of his mind—those charioteers who hale
Might-without-right behind them: face who can
Fortune's reverse which time prepares, nor quail?
—He who evades law and in lawlessness
Delights him,—he has broken down his trust—
The chariot, riches haled—now blackening in the dust!

Ismenos, go thou garlanded!
Break into dance, ye ways, the polished bed
O' the seven-gated city! Dirké, thou
Fair-flowing, with the Asopiad sisters all,
Leave your sire's stream, attend the festival
Of Herakles, one choir of nymphs, sing triumph now!
O woody rock of Puthios and each home
O the Helikonian Muses, ye shall come
With joyous shouting to my walls, my town
Where saw the light that Spartan race, those "Sown,"
Brazen-shield-bearing chiefs, whereof the band
With children's children renovates our land,
To Thebes a sacred light!
O combination of the marriage rite—
Bed of the mortal-born and Zeus, who couched
Beside the nymph of Perseus' progeny!
For credible, past hope, becomes to me
That nuptial story long ago avouched,
O Zeus! and time has turned the dark to bright,
And made one blaze of truth the Herakleidan might—
His, who emerged from earth's pavilion, left
Plouton's abode, the nether palace-cleft,
Thou wast the lord that nature gave me—not
That baseness born and bred—my king, by lot!
—Baseness made plain to all, who now regard
The match of sword with sword in fight,—
If to the gods the Just and Right
Still pleasing be, still claim the palm's award.

Horror!
Are we come to the selfsame passion of fear,
Old friends?—such a phantasm fronts me here
Visible over the palace-roof!
In flight, in flight, the laggard limb
Bestir! and haste aloof
From that on the roof there—grand and grim!
O Paian, king!
Be thou my safeguard from the woeful thing!

IRIS

Courage, old men! beholding here—Night's birth—
Madness, and me the handmaid of the gods,
Iris: since to your town we come, no plague—
Wage war against the house of but one man
From Zeus and from Alkmené sprung, they say.
Now, till he made an end of bitter toils,
Fate kept him safe, nor did his father Zeus
Let us once hurt him, Heré nor myself.
But, since he has toiled through Eurustheus' task,
Heré desires to fix fresh blood on him—
Slaying his children: I desire it too.

Up then, collecting the unsoftened heart,
Unwedded virgin of black Night! Drive, drag
Frenzy upon the man here—whirls of brain
Big with child-murder, while his feet leap gay!
Let go the bloody cable its whole length!
So that,—when o'er the Acherousian ford
He has sent floating, by self-homicide,
His beautiful boy-garland,—he may know
First, Heré's anger, what it is to him,
And then learn mine. The gods are vile indeed
And mortal matters vast, if he 'scape free!

MADNESS

Certes, from well-born sire and mother too
Had I my birth, whose blood is Night's and Heaven's;
But here's my glory,—not to grudge the good!
Nor love I raids against the friends of man.
I wish, then, to persuade,—before I see
You stumbling, you and Heré! trust my words!
This man, the house of whom ye hound me to,
Is not unfamed on earth nor gods among;
Since, having quelled waste land and savage sea,
He alone raised again the falling rights
Of gods—gone ruinous through impious men.
Desire no mighty mischief, I advise!

IRIS

Give thou no thought to Heré's faulty schemes!

MADNESS

Changing her step from faulty to fault-free!

IRIS

Not to be wise, did Zeus' wife send thee here!

MADNESS

Sun, thee I cite to witness—doing what I loathe to do!
But since indeed to Heré and thyself I must subserve.
And follow you quick, with a whiz, as the hounds a-hunt with the huntsman,
—Go I will! and neither the sea, as it groans with its waves so furiously,
Nor earthquake, no, nor the bolt of thunder gasping out heaven's labor-throe,
Shall cover the ground as I, at a bound, rush into the bosom of Herakles!
And home I scatter, and house I batter,
Having first of all made the children fall,—
And he who felled them is never to know
He gave birth to each child that received the blow,
Till the Madness, I am, have let him go!

Ha, behold, already he rocks his head—he is off from the starting-place!
Not a word, as he rolls his frightful orbs, from their sockets wrenched in the ghastly race!
And the breathings of him he tempers and times no more than a bull in act to toss,
And hideously he bellows invoking the Keres, daughters of Tartaros.
Ay, and I soon will dance thee madder, and pipe thee quite out of thy mind with fear!
So, up with the famous foot, thou Iris, march to Olumpos, leave me here!
Me and mine, who now combine, in the dreadful shape no mortal sees,
And now are about to pass, from without, inside of the home of Herakles!

CHOROS

Otototoi,—groan! Away is mown
Thy flower, Zeus' offspring, City!
Unhappy Hellas, who dost cast (the pity!)
Who worked thee all the good,
Away from thee,—destroyest in a mood
Of madness him, to death whom pipings dance!
There goes she, in her chariot—groans, her brood—
And gives her team the goad, as though adrift
For doom, Night's Gorgon, Madness, she whose glance
Turns man to marble! with what hissings lift
Their hundred heads the snakes, her head's inheritance!
Quick has the god changed fortune: through their sire
Quick will the children, that he saved, expire!
O miserable me! O Zeus! thy child—
Childless himself—soon vengeance, hunger-wild,
Craving for punishment, will lay how low—
Loaded with many a woe!

O palace-roofs! your courts about,
A measure begins all unrejoiced
By the tympanies and the thyrsos hoist
Of the Bromian revel-rout!
O ye domes! and the measure proceeds
For blood, not such as the cluster bleeds

Of the Dionusian pouring-out!

Break forth, fly, children! fatal this—
Fatal the lay that is piped, I wis!
Ay, for he hunts a children-chase—
Never shall Madness lead her revel
And leave no trace in the dwelling-place!
Ai ai, because of the evil!
Ai ai, the old man—how I groan
For the father, and not the father alone!
She who was nurse of his children,—small
Her gain that they ever were born at all!

See! See!
A whirlwind shakes hither and thither
The house—the roof falls in together!
Ha, ha! what dost thou, son of Zeus?
A trouble of Tartaros broke loose,
Such as once Pallas on the Titan thundered,
Thou sendest on thy domes, roof-shattered and wall-sundered!

MESSENGER
O bodies white with age!—

CHOROS
What cry, to me—
What, dost thou call with?

MESSENGER
There 's a curse indoors!

CHOROS
I shall not bring a prophet: you suffice!

MESSENGER
Dead are the children!

CHOROS
Ai ai!

MESSENGER
Groan! for, groans
Suit well the subject! Dire the children's death,
Dire too the parent's hands that dealt the fate.
No one could tell worse woe than we have borne!

CHOROS
How dost thou that same curse—curse, cause for groan

The father's on the children, make appear?
Tell in what matter they were hurled from heaven
Against the house—these evils; and recount
The children's hapless fate, O Messenger!

MESSENGER
The victims were before the hearth of Zeus
A household-expiation: since the king
O' the country, Herakles had killed and cast
From out the dwelling; and a beauteous choir
Of boys stood by his sire, too, and his wife.
And now the basket had been carried round
The altar in a circle, and we used
The consecrated speech. Alkmené's son—
Just as he was about, in his right hand,
To bear the torch, that he might dip into
The cleansing-water—came to a stand-still;
And, as their father yet delayed, his boys
Had their eyes on him. But he was himself
No longer: lost in rollings of the eyes;
Out-thrusting eyes—their very roots—like blood!
Froth he dropped down his bushy-bearded cheek,
And said—together with a madman's laugh—
"Father! why sacrifice, before I slay
Eurustheus? why have twice the lustral fire,
And double pains, when 't is permitted me
To end, with one good hand-sweep, matters here?
Then,—when I hither bring Eurustheus' head,—
Then for these just slain, wash hands once for all!
Now,—cast drink-offerings forth, throw baskets down!
Who gives me bow and arrows, who my club?
I go to that Mukenai! One must match
Crowbars and mattocks, so that—those sunk stones
The Kuklops squared with picks and plumb-line red.
I, with my bent steel, may o'ertumble town!"
Which said, he goes and—with no car to have—
Affirms he has one! mounts the chariot-board,
And strikes, as having really goad in hand!
And two ways laughed the servants—laugh with awe;
And one said, as each met the other's stare,
"Playing us boys' tricks? or is master mad?"
But up he climbs, and down along the roof,
And, dropping into the men's place, maintains
He 's come to Nisos city, when he 's come
Only inside his own house! then reclines
On floor, for couch, and, as arrived indeed,
Makes himself supper; goes through some brief stay,
Then says he 's traversing the forest-flats

Of Isthmos; thereupon lays body bare
Of bucklings, and begins a contest with
—No one! and is proclaimed the conqueror—
He by himself—having called out to hear
—Nobody! Then, if you will take his word,
Blaring against Eurustheus horribly,
He 's at Mukenai. But his father laid
Hold of the strong hand and addressed him thus:
"O son, what ails thee? Of what sort is this
Extravagance? Has not some murder-craze,
Bred of those corpses thou didst just dispatch,
Danced thee drunk?" But he,—taking him to crouch,
Eurustheus' sire, that apprehensive touched
His hand, a suppliant,—pushes him aside,
Gets ready quiver, and bends low against
His children—thinking them Eurustheus' boys
He means to slay. They, horrified with fear,
Rushed here and there,—this child, into the robes
O' the wretched mother,—this, beneath the shade
O' the column,—and this other, like a bird,
Cowered at the altar-foot. The mother shrieks,
"Parent—what dost thou?—kill thy children?" So
Shriek the old sire and crowd of servitors.
But he, outwinding him, as round about
The column ran the boy,—a horrid whirl
O' the lathe his foot described!—stands opposite,
Strikes through the liver! and supine the boy
Bedews the stone shafts, breathing out his life.
But "Victory" he shouted! boasted thus:
"Well, this one nestling of Eurustheus—dead—
Falls by me, pays back the paternal hate!"
Then bends bow on another who was crouched
At base of altar—overlooked, he thought—
And now prevents him, falls at father's knee,
Throwing up hand to beard and cheek above.
"O dearest!" cries he, "father, kill me not!
Yours, I am—your boy: not Eurustheus' boy
You kill now!" But he, rolling the wild eye
Of Gorgon,—as the boy stood all too close
For deadly bowshot,—mimicry of smith
Who batters red-hot iron,—hand o'er head
Heaving his club, on the boy's yellow hair
Hurls it and breaks the bone. This second caught,—
He goes, would slay the third, one sacrifice
He and the couple; but, beforehand here,
The miserable mother catches up,
Carries him inside house and bars the gate.
Then he, as he were at those Kuklops' work,

Digs at, heaves doors up, wrenches doorposts out,
Lays wife and child low with the selfsame shaft.
And this done, at the old man's death he drives;
But there came, as it seemed to us who saw,
A statue—Pallas with the crested head,
Swinging her spear—and threw a stone which smote
Herakles' breast and stayed his slaughter-rage,
And sent him safe to sleep. He falls to ground—
Striking against the column with his back—
Column which, with the falling of the roof,
Broken in two, lay by the altar-base.
And we, foot-free now from our several flights,
Along with the old man, we fastened bonds
Of rope-noose to the column, so that he,
Ceasing from sleep, might not go adding deeds
To deeds done. And he sleeps a sleep, poor wretch,
No gift of any god! since he has slain
Children and wife. For me, I do not know
What mortal has more misery to bear.

CHOROS

A murder there was which Argolis
Holds in remembrance, Hellas through,
As, at that time, best and famousest:
Of those, the daughters of Danaos slew.
A murder indeed was that! but this
Outstrips it, straight to the goal has pressed.
I am able to speak of a murder done
To the hapless Zeus-born offspring, too—
Proknè's son, who had but one—
Or a sacrifice to the Muses, say
Rather, who Itus sing alway,
Her single child! But thou, the sire
Of children three—O thou consuming fire!—
In one outrageous fate hast made them all expire!
And this outrageous fate—
What groan, or wail, or deadmen's dirge,
Or choric dance of Haides shall I urge
The Muse to celebrate?

Woe! woe! behold!
The portalled palace lies unrolled,
This way and that way, each prodigious fold!
Alas for me! these children, see,
Stretched, hapless group, before their father—he
The all-unhappy, who lies sleeping out
The murder of his sons, a dreadful sleep!
And bonds, see, all about,—

Rope-tangle, ties and tether,—these
Tightenings around the body of Herakles
To the stone columns of the house made fast!

But—like a bird that grieves
For callow nestlings some rude hand bereaves—
See, here, a bitter journey overpast,
The old man—all too late—is here at last!

AMPHITRUON
Silently, silently, aged Kadmeians!
Will ye not suffer my son, diffused
Yonder, to slide from his sorrows in sleep?

CHOROS
And thee, old man, do I, groaning, weep,
And the children too, and the head there—used
Of old to the wreaths and paians!

AMPHITRUON
Farther away! Nor beat the breast,
Nor wail aloud, nor rouse from rest
The slumberer—asleep, so best!

CHOROS
Ah me—what a slaughter!

AMPHITRUON
Refrain—refrain!
Ye will prove my perdition!

CHOROS
Unlike water,
Bloodshed rises from earth again!

AMPHITRUON
Do I bid you bate your breath, in vain—
Ye elders? Lament in a softer strain!
Lest he rouse himself, burst every chain,
And bury the city in ravage—bray
Father and house to dust away!

CHOROS
I cannot forbear—I cannot forbear!

AMPHITRUON
Hush! I will learn his breathings: there!
I will lay my ears close.

CHOROS

What, he sleeps?

AMPHITRUON

Ay,—sleeps! A horror of slumber keeps
The man who has piled
On wife and child
Death and death, as he shot them down
With clang o'the bow.

CHOROS

Wail—

AMPHITRUON

Even so!

CHOROS

—The fate of the children—

AMPHITRUON

Triple woe!

CHOROS

—Old man, the fate of thy son!

AMPHITRUON

Hush, hush! Have done!
He is turning about!
He is breaking out!
Away! I steal
And my body conceal,
Before he arouse,
In the depths of the house!

CHOROS

Courage! The Night
Maintains her right
On the lids of thy son there, sealed from sight!

AMPHITRUON

See, see! To leave the light
And, wretch that I am, bear one last ill,
I do not avoid; but if he kill
Me, his own father, and devise
Beyond the present miseries
A misery more ghastly still—
And to haunt him, over and above

Those here who, as they used to love,
Now hate him, what if he have with these
My murder, the worst of Erinues?

CHOROS

Then was the time to die, for thee,
When ready to wreak in the full degree
Vengeance on those
Thy consort's foes
Who murdered her brothers! glad, life's close,
With the Taphioi down,
And sacked their town
Clustered about with a wash of sea!

AMPHITRUON

Tonight—to flight!
Away from the house, troop off, old men!
Save yourselves out of the maniac's sight!
He is rousing himself right up: and then,
Murder on murder heaping anew,
He will revel in blood your city through!

CHOROS

O Zeus, why hast, with such unmeasured hate,
Hated thy son, whelmed in this sea of woes?

HERAKLES

Ha,—
In breath indeed I am—see things I ought—
Æther, and earth, and these the sunbeam-shafts!
But then—some billow and strange whirl of sense
I have fallen into! and breathings hot I breathe—
Smoked upwards, not the steady work from lungs.
See now! Why, bound—at moorings like a ship,—
About my young breast and young arm, to this
Stone piece of carved work broke in half, do I
Sit, have my rest in corpses' neighborhood?
Strewn on the ground are wingèd darts, and bow
Which played, my brother-shieldman, held in hand,—
Guarded my side, and got my guardianship!
I cannot have gone back to Haides—twice.
Begun Eurustheus' race I ended thence?
But I nor see the Sisupheian stone,
Nor Plouton, nor Demeter's sceptred maid!
I am struck witless sure! Where can I be?
Ho there! what friend of mine is near or far—
Some one to cure me of bewilderment?
For naught familiar do I recognize.

AMPHITRUON
Old friends, shall I go close to these my woes?

CHOROS
Ay, and let me too,—nor desert your ills!

HERAKLES
Father, why weepest thou, and buriest up
Thine eyes, aloof so from thy much-loved son?

AMPHITRUON
O child!—for, faring badly, mine thou art!

HERAKLES
Do I fare somehow ill, that tears should flow?

AMPHITRUON
Ill,—would cause any god who bore to groan!

HERAKLES
That's boasting, truly! still, you state no hap.

AMPHITRUON
For, thyself seest—if in thy wits again.

HERAKLES
Heyday! How riddlingly that hint returns!

AMPHITRUON
Well, I am trying—art thou sane and sound!

HERAKLES
Say if thou lay'st aught strange to my life's charge!

AMPHITRUON
If thou no more art Haides-drunk,—I tell!

HERAKLES
I bring to mind no drunkenness of soul.

AMPHITRUON
Shall I unbind my son, old men, or what?

HERAKLES
And who was binder, tell!—not that, my deed!

AMPHITRUON

Mind that much of misfortune—pass the rest!

HERAKLES
Enough! from silence, I nor learn nor wish.

AMPHITRUON
O Zeus, dost witness here throned Heré's work?

HERAKLES
But have I had to bear aught hostile thence?

AMPHITRUON
Let be the goddess—bury thine own guilt!

HERAKLES
Undone! What is the sorrow thou wilt say?

AMPHITRUON
Look! See the ruins of thy children here!

HERAKLES
Ah me! What sight do wretched I behold?

AMPHITRUON
Unfair fight, son, this fight thou fastenedst
On thine own children!

HERAKLES
What fight? Who slew these?

AMPHITRUON
Thou and thy bow, and who of gods was cause.

HERAKLES
How say'st? What did I? Ill-announcing sire!

AMPHITRUON
—Go mad! Thou askest a sad clearing up!

HERAKLES
And am I also murderer of my wife?

AMPHITRUON
All the work here was just one hand's work—thine!

HERAKLES
Ai ai—for groans encompass me—a cloud!

AMPHITRUON

For these deeds' sake do I begroan thy fate!

HERAKLES

Did I break up my house or dance it down?

AMPHITRUON

I know just one thing—all 's a woe with thee!

HERAKLES

But where did the craze catch me, where destroy?

AMPHITRUON

When thou didst cleanse hands at the altar-flame.

HERAKLES

Ah me! why is it then I save my life—
Proved murderer of my dearest ones, my boys?
Shall not I rush to the rock-level's leap,
Or, darting sword through breast and all, become
My children's blood-avenger? or, this flesh
Burning away with fire, so thrust away
The infamy, which waits me there, from life?
Ah, but,—a hindrance to my purposed death,
Theseus arrives, my friend and kinsman, here!
Eyes will be on me! my child-murder-plague
In evidence before friends loved so much!
O me, what shall I do? Where, taking wing
Or gliding underground, shall I seek out
A solitariness from misery?
I will pull night upon my muffled head!
Let this wretch here content him with his curse
Of blood: I would pollute no innocents!

THESEUS

I come,—with others who await beside
Asopos' stream, the armed Athenian youth,—
Bring thy son, old man, spear's fight-fellowship!
For a bruit reached the Erechtheidai's town
That, having seized the sceptre of this realm,
Lukos prepares you battle-violence.
So, paying good back,—Herakles began,
Saving me down there,—I have come, old man,
If aught, of my hand or my friends', you want.
What 's here? Why all these corpses on the ground?
Am I perhaps behindhand—come too late
For newer ill? Who killed these children now?
Whose wife was she, this woman I behold?

Boys, at least, take no stand in reach of spear!
Some other woe than war, I chance upon!

AMPHITRUON
O thou, who sway'st the olive-bearing height!—

THESEUS
Why hail'st thou me with woeful prelude thus?

AMPHITRUON
Dire sufferings have we suffered from the gods.

THESEUS
These boys,—who are they, thou art weeping o'er?

AMPHITRUON
He gave them birth, indeed, my hapless son!
Begot, but killed them—dared their bloody death.

THESEUS
Speak no such horror!

AMPHITRUON
Would I might obey!

THESEUS
O teller of dread tidings!

AMPHITRUON
Lost are we—
Lost—flown away from life!

THESEUS
What sayest thou?
What did he?

AMPHITRUON
Erring through a frenzy-fit,
He did all, with the arrows dipt in dye
Of hundred-headed Hudra.

THESEUS
Heré 's strife!
But who is this among the dead, old man?

AMPHITRUON
Mine, mine, this progeny—the labor-plagued,
Who went with gods once to Phlegruia's plain.

And in the giant-slaying war bore shield!

THESEUS
Woe—woe! What man was born mischanceful thus!

AMPHITRUON
Thou couldst not know another mortal man
Toil-weary, more outworn by wanderings.

THESEUS
And why i' the peploi hides he his sad head?

AMPHITRUON
Not daring meet thine eye, thy friendliness
And kinship,—nor that children's—blood about!

THESEUS
But I come to who shared my woe with me!
Uncover him!

AMPHITRUON
O child, put from thine eyes
The peplos, throw it off, show face to sun!
Woe's weight well matched contends with tears in thee.
I supplicate thee, falling at thy cheek
And knee and hand, and shedding this old tear!
O son, remit the savage lion's mood,
Since to a bloody, an unholy race
Art thou led forth, if thou be resolute
To go on adding ill to ill, my child!

THESEUS
Let me speak! Thee, who sittest—seated woe—
I call upon to show thy friends thine eye!
For there 's no darkness has a cloud so black
May hide thy misery thus absolute.
Why, waving hand, dost sign me—murder 's done?
Lest a pollution strike me, from thy speech?
Naught care I to—with thee, at least—fare ill:
For I had joy once! Then,—soul rises to,—
When thou didst save me from the dead to light!
Friends' gratitude that tastes old age, I loathe,
And him who likes to share when things look fine,
But, sail along with friends in trouble—no!
Arise, uncover thine unhappy head!
Look on us! Every man of the right race
Bears what, at least, the gods inflict, nor shrinks.

HERAKLES

Theseus, hast seen this match—my boys with me?

THESEUS

I heard of, now I see the ills thou sign'st.

HERAKLES

Why then hast thou displayed my head to sun?

THESEUS

Why? mortals bring no plague on aught divine!

HERAKLES

Fly, O unhappy, this my impious plague!

THESEUS

No plague of vengeance flits to friends from friends.

HERAKLES

I praise thee! But I helped thee,—that is truth.

THESEUS

And I, advantaged then, now pity thee.

HERAKLES

—The pitiable,—my children's murderer!

THESEUS

I mourn for thy sake, in this altered lot.

HERAKLES

Hast thou found others in still greater woe?

THESEUS

Thou, from earth, touchest heaven, one huge distress!

HERAKLES

Accordingly, I am prepared to die.

THESEUS

Think'st thou thy threats at all import the gods?

HERAKLES

Gods please themselves: to gods I give their like.

THESEUS

Shut thy mouth, lest big words bring bigger woe!

HERAKLES

I am full fraught with ills—no stowing more!

THESEUS

Thou wilt do—what, then? Whither moody borne?

HERAKLES

Dying, I go below earth whence I came.

THESEUS

Thou hast used words of—what man turns up first!

HERAKLES

While thou, being outside sorrow, schoolest me.

THESEUS

The much-enduring Herakles talks thus?—

HERAKLES

Not the so much-enduring: measure's past!

THESEUS

—Mainstay to mortals, and their mighty friend?

HERAKLES

They nowise profit me: but Heré rules.

THESEUS

Hellas forbids thou shouldst ineptly die.

HERAKLES

But hear, then, how I strive by arguments
Against thy teachings! I will ope thee out
My life—past, present—as unlivable.
First, I was born of this man, who had slain
His mother's aged sire, and, sullied so,
Married Alkmené, she who gave me birth.
Now, when the basis of a family
Is not laid right, what follows needs must fall;
And Zeus, whoever Zeus is, formed me foe
To Heré (take not thou offence, old man!
Since father, in Zeus' stead, account I thee)
And, while I was at suck yet, frightful snakes
She introduced among my swaddling-clothes,—
That bedfellow of Zeus!—to end me so.
But when I gained the youthful garb of flesh,
The labors I endured—what need to tell?
What lions ever, or three-bodied brutes,

Tuphons or giants, or the four-legg'd swarms
Of Kentaur-battle, did not I end out?
And that hound, headed all about with heads
Which cropped up twice, the Hudra, having slain—
I both went through a myriad other toils
In full drove, and arrived among the dead
To convoy, as Eurustheus bade, to light
Haides' three-headed dog and doorkeeper.
But then I,—wretch,—dared this last labor—see!
Slew my sons, keystone-coped my house with ills,
To such a strait I come! nor my dear Thebes
Dare I inhabit,—and, suppose I stay?
Into what fane or festival of friends
Am I to go? My curse scarce courts accost!
Shall I seek Argos? How, if fled from home?
But say,—I hurry to some other town!
And there they eye me, as notorious now,—
Kept by sharp tongue-taunts under lock and key—
"Is not this he, Zeus' son, who murdered once
Children and wife? Let him go rot elsewhere!"
To any man renowned as happy once,
Reverses are a grave thing; but to whom
Evil is old acquaintance, there 's no hurt
To speak of, he and misery are twins.
To this degree of woe I think to come:
For earth will utter voice forbidding me
To touch the ground, and sea—to pierce the wave,
The river-springs—to drink, and I shall play
Ixion's part quite out, the chained and wheeled!
And best of all will be, if so I 'scape
Sight from one man of those Hellenes,—once
I lived among, felicitous and rich!
Why ought I then to live? What gain accrues
From good-for-nothing, wicked life I lead?
In fine, let Zeus' brave consort dance and sing,
Stamp foot, the Olumpian Zeus' own sandal-trick!
What she has willed, that brings her will to pass—
The foremost man of Hellas pedestalled,
Up, over, and down whirling! Who would pray
To such a goddess?—that, begrudging Zeus
Because he loved a woman, ruins me—
Lover of Hellas, faultless of the wrong!

THESEUS
This strife is from no other of the gods
Than Zeus' wife; rightly apprehend, as well,
Why, to no death—thou meditatest now—
I would persuade thee, but to bear thy woes!

None, none of mortals boasts a fate unmixed,
Nor gods—if poets' teaching be not false.
Have not they joined in wedlock against law
With one another? not, for sake of rule,
Branded their sires in bondage? Yet they house,
All the same, in Olumpos, carry heads
High there, notorious sinners though they be!
What wilt thou say, then, if thou, mortal-born,
Bearest outrageously fate gods endure?
Leave Thebes, now, pay obedience to the law,
And follow me to Pallas' citadel!
There, when thy hands are purified from stain,
House will I give thee, and goods shared alike.
What gifts I hold too from the citizens
For saving twice seven children, when I slew
The Knosian bull, these also give I thee.
And everywhere about the land are plots
Apportioned me: these, named by thine own name,
Shall be henceforward styled by all men—thine,
Thy life-long; but at death, when Haides-bound,
All Athens shall uphold the honored one
With sacrifices, and huge marble heaps:
For that's a fair crown our Hellenes grant
Their people—glory, should they help the brave!
And I repay thee back this grace for thine
That saved me, now that thou art lorn of friends—
Since, when the gods give honor, friends may flit:
For, a god's help suffices, if he please.

HERAKLES
Ah me, these words are foreign to my woes!
I neither fancy gods love lawless beds,
Nor, that with chains they bind each other's hands,
Have I judged worthy faith, at any time;
Nor shall I be persuaded—one is born
His fellows' master! since God stands in need—
If he is really God—of naught at all.
These are the poets' pitiful conceits!
But this it was I pondered, though woe-whelmed—
"Take heed lest thou be taxed with cowardice
Somehow in leaving thus the light of day!"
For whoso cannot make a stand against
These same misfortunes, neither could withstand
A mere man's dart, oppose death, strength to strength.
Therefore unto thy city I will go
And have the grace of thy ten thousand gifts.
There! I have tasted of ten thousand toils
As truly—never waived a single one,

Nor let these runnings drop from out my eyes!
Nor ever thought it would have come to this—
That I from out my eyes do drop tears! Well!
At present, as it seems, one bows to fate.
So be it! Old man, thou seest my exile—
Seest, too, me—my children's murderer!
These give thou to the tomb, and deck the dead,
Doing them honor with thy tears—since me
Law does not sanction! Propping on her breast,
And giving them into their mother's arms,
—Reinstitute the sad community
Which I, unhappy, brought to nothingness—
Not by my will! And, when earth hides the dead,
Live in this city!—sad, but, all the same,
Force thy soul to bear woe along with me!
O children, who begat and gave you birth—
Your father—has destroyed you! naught you gain
By those fair deeds of mine I laid you up,
As by main-force I labored glory out
To give you,—that fine gift of fatherhood!
And thee, too, O my poor one, I destroyed.
Not rendering like for like, as when thou kept'st
My marriage-bed inviolate,—those long
Household-seclusions draining to the dregs
Inside my house! O me, my wife, my boys—
And—O myself, how, miserably moved.
Am I disyoked now from both boys and wife!
Oh, bitter those delights of kisses now—
And bitter these my weapons' fellowship!
For I am doubtful whether shall I keep
Or cast away these arrows which will clang
Ever such words out, as they knock my side—
"Us—thou didst murder wife and children with!
Us—child—destroyers—still thou keepest thine!"
Ha, shall I bear them in my arms, then? What
Say for excuse? Yet, naked of my darts
Wherewith I did my bravest, Hellas through,
Throwing myself beneath foot to my foes,
Shall I die basely? No! relinquishment
Of these must never be,—companions once,
We sorrowfully must observe the pact!
In just one thing, co-operate with me
Thy sad friend, Theseus! Go along with him
To Argos, and in concert get arranged
The price my due for bringing there the Hound!
O land of Kadmos, Theban people all,
Shear off your locks, lament one wide lament,
Go to my children's grave and, in one strain,

Lament the whole of us—my dead and me—
Since all together are foredone and lost,
Smitten by Herd's single stroke of fate!

THESEUS
Rise up now from thy dead ones! Tears enough,
Poor friend!

HERAKLES
I cannot: for my limbs are fixed.

THESEUS
Ay: even these strong men fate overthrows!

HERAKLES
Woe!
Here might I grow a stone, nor mind woes more!

THESEUS
Cease! Give thy hand to friendly helpmate now!

HERAKLES
Nay, but I wipe off blood upon thy robes!

THESEUS
Squeeze out and spare no drop! I take it all!

HERAKLES
Of sons bereaved, I have thee like my son!

THESEUS
Give to my neck thy hand! 'tis I will lead.

HERAKLES
Yoke-fellows friendly—one heartbroken, though!
O father! such a man we need for friend!

AMPHITRUON
Certes, the land that bred him boasts good sons!

HERAKLES
Turn me round, Theseus—to behold my boys!

THESEUS
What? will the having such a love-charm soothe?

HERAKLES
I want it; and to press my father's breast.

AMPHITRUON
See here, O son! for, what I love thou seek'st!

THESEUS
Strange! Of thy labors no more memory?

HERAKLES
All those were less than these, those ills I bore!

THESEUS
Who sees thee grow a woman,—will not praise!

HERAKLES
I live low to thee? Not so once, I think!

THESEUS
Too low by far! "Famed Herakles"—where 's he?

HERAKLES
Down amid evils, of what kind wast thou?

THESEUS
As far as courage—least of all mankind!

HERAKLES
How say'st, then, I in evils shrink to naught?

THESEUS
Forward!

HERAKLES
Farewell, old father!

AMPHITRUON
Thou too, son!

HERAKLES
Bury the boys as I enjoined!

AMPHITRUON
And me—
Who will be found to bury now, my child?

HERAKLES
Myself!

AMPHITRUON

When, coming?

HERAKLES
When thy task is done.

AMPHITRUON
How?

HERAKLES
I will have thee carried forth from Thebes
To Athens. But bear in the children, earth
Is burdened by! Myself,—who with these shames
Have cast away my house,—a ruined hulk,
I follow—trailed by Theseus—on my way;
And whoso rather would have wealth and strength
Than good friends, reasons foolishly therein!

CHOROS
And we depart, with sorrow at heart,
Sobs that increase with tears that start;
The greatest of all our friends of yore
We have lost forevermore!

When the long silence ended,—"Our best friend—
Lost, our best friend!" he muttered musingly.
Then, "Lachares the sculptor" (half aloud)
"Sinned he or sinned he not? 'Outrageous sin!'
Shuddered our elders, 'Pallas should be clothed:
He carved her naked.' 'But more beautiful!'
Answers this generation: 'Wisdom formed
For love not fear!' And there the statue stands,
Entraps the eye severer art repels.
Moreover, Pallas wields the thunderbolt,
Yet has not struck the artist all this while.
Pheidias and Aischulos? Euripides
And Lachares? But youth will have its way!
The ripe man ought to be as old as young—
As young as old. I too have youth at need.
Much may be said for stripping wisdom bare!

"And who 's 'our best friend'? You play kottabos;
Here 's the last mode of playing. Take a sphere
With orifices at due interval,
Through topmost one of which, a throw adroit
Sends wine from cup, clean passage, from outside
To where, in hollow midst, a manikin
Suspended ever bobs with head erect

Right underneath whatever hole 's a-top
When you set orb a-rolling: plumb, he gets
Ever this benediction of the splash.
An other-fashioned orb presents him fixed:
Of all the outlets, he fronts only one,
And only when that one—and rare the chance—
Comes uppermost, does he turn upward too:
He can't turn all sides with the turning orb.
Inside this sphere of life—all objects, sense
And soul perceive—Euripides hangs fixed,
Gets knowledge through the single aperture
Of High and Right: with visage fronting these
He waits the wine thence ere he operate,
Work in the world and write a tragedy.
When that hole happens to revolve to point,
In drops the knowledge, waiting meets reward.
But, duly in rotation, Low and Wrong—
When these enjoy the moment's altitude,
His heels are found just where his head should be!
No knowledge that way! I am movable,—
To slightest shift of orb make prompt response,
Face Low and Wrong and Weak and all the rest,
And still drink knowledge, wine-drenched every turn,—
Equally favored by their opposites.
Little and Bad exist, are natural:
Then let me know them, and be twice as great
As he who only knows one phase of life!
So doubly shall I prove 'best friend of man,'
If I report the whole truth—Vice, perceived
While he shut eyes to all but Virtue there.
Man 's made of both: and both must be of use
To somebody: if not to him, to me.
While, as to your imaginary Third,
Who,—stationed (by mechanics past my guess)
So as to take in every side at once,
And not successively,—may reconcile
The High and Low in tragicomic verse,—
He shall be hailed superior to us both
When born—in the Tin-islands! Meantime, here
In bright Athenai, I contest the claim,
Call myself Iostephanos' 'best friend,'
Who took my own course, worked as I descried
Ordainment, stuck to my first faculty!

"For, listen! There 's no failure breaks the heart,
Whate'er be man's endeavor in this world,
Like the rash poet's when he—nowise fails
By poetizing badly,—Zeus or makes

Or mars a man, so—at it, merrily!
But when,—made man,—much like myself,—equipt
For such and such achievement,—rash he turns
Out of the straight path, bent on snatch of feat
From—who 's the appointed fellow born thereto,—
Crows take him!—in your Kassiterides?
Half-doing his work, leaving mine untouched,
That were the failure! Here I stand, heart-whole,
No Thamuris!

"Well thought of, Thamuris!
Has zeal, pray, for 'best friend' Euripides
Allowed you to observe the honor done
His elder rival, in our Poikilé?
You don't know? Once and only once, trod stage,
Sang and touched lyre in person, in his youth,
Our Sophokles,—youth, beauty, dedicate
To Thamuris who named the tragedy.
The voice of him was weak; face, limbs and lyre,
These were worth saving: Thamuris stands yet
Perfect as painting helps in such a case.
At least you know the story, for 'best friend'
Enriched his 'Rhesos' from the Blind Bard's store;
So haste and see the work, and lay to heart
What it was struck me when I eyed the piece!
Here stands a poet punished for rash strife
With Powers above his power, who see with sight
Beyond his vision, sing accordingly
A song, which he must needs dare emulate!
Poet, remain the man nor ape the Muse!

"But—lend me the psalterion! Nay, for once—
Once let my hand fall where the other's lay!
I see it, just as I were Sophokles,
That sunrise and combustion of the east!"

And then he sang—are these unlike the words?

Thamuris marching,—lyre and song of Thrace—
(Perpend the first, the worst of woes that were,
Allotted lyre and song, ye poet-race!)

Thamuris from Oichalia, feasted there
By kingly Eurutos of late, now bound
For Dorion at the uprise broad and bare

Of Mount Pangaios (ore with earth enwound
Glittered beneath his footstep)—marching gay

And glad, Thessalia through, came, robed and crowned,

From triumph on to triumph, 'mid a ray
Of early morn,—came, saw and knew the spot
Assigned him for his worst of woes, that day.

Balura—happier while its name was not—
Met him, but nowise menaced; slipt aside,
Obsequious river, to pursue its lot

Of solacing the valley—say, some wide
Thick busy human cluster, house and home,
Embanked for peace, or thrift that thanks the tide.

Thamuris, marching, laughed "Each flake of foam"
(As sparklingly the ripple raced him by)
"Mocks slower clouds adrift in the blue dome!"

For Autumn was the season: red the sky
Held morn's conclusive signet of the sun
To break the mists up, bid them blaze and die.

Morn had the mastery as, one by one,
All pomps produced themselves along the tract
From earth's far ending to near heaven begun.

Was there a ravaged tree? it laughed compact
With gold, a leaf-ball crisp, high-brandished now,
Tempting to onset frost which late attacked.

Was there a wizened shrub, a starveling bough,
A fleecy thistle filched from by the wind,
A weed, Pan's trampling hoof would disallow?

Each, with a glory and a rapture twined
About it, joined the rush of air and light
And force: the world was of one joyous mind.

Say not the birds flew! they forebore their right—
Swam, revelling onward in the roll of things.
Say not the beasts' mirth bounded! that was flight—

How could the creatures leap, no lift of wings?
Such earth's community of purpose, such
The ease of earth's fulfilled imaginings,—

So did the near and far appear to touch
I' the moment's transport,—that an interchange

Of function, far with near, seemed scarce too much;

And had the rooted plant aspired to range
With the snake's license, while the insect yearned
To glow fixed as the flower it were not strange—

No more than if the fluttery tree-top turned
To actual music, sang itself aloft;
Or if the wind, impassioned chantress, earned

The right to soar embodied in some soft
Fine form all fit for cloud-companionship,
And, blissful, once touch beauty chased so oft.

Thamuris, marching, let no fancy slip
Born of the fiery transport; lyre and song
Were his, to smite with hand and launch from lip—

Peerless recorded, since the list grew long
Of poets (saith Homeros) free to stand
Pedestalled 'mid the Muses' temple-throng,

A statued service, laurelled, lyre in hand,
(Ay, for we see them)—Thamuris of Thrace
Predominating foremost of the band.

Therefore the morn-ray that enriched his face,
If it gave lambent chill, took flame again
From flush of pride; he saw, he knew the place.

What wind arrived with all the rhythms from plain,
Hill, dale, and that rough wildwood interspersed?
Compounding these to one consummate strain,

It reached him, music; but his own outburst
Of victory concluded the account,
And that grew song which was mere music erst.

"Be my Parnassos, thou Pangaian mount!
And turn thee, river, nameless hitherto!
Famed shalt thou vie with famed Pieria's fount!

Here I await the end of this ado:
Which wins—Earth's poet or the Heavenly Muse." ...

But song broke up in laughter. "Tell the rest,
Who may! I have not spurned the common life,
Nor vaunted mine a lyre to match the Muse

Who sings for gods, not men! Accordingly,
I shall not decorate her vestibule—
Mute marble, blind the eyes and quenched the brain,
Loose in the hand a bright, a broken lyre!
—Not Thamuris but Aristophanes!

"There! I have sung content back to myself,
And started subject for a play beside.
My next performance shall content you both.
Did 'Prelude-Battle' maul 'best friend' too much?
Then 'Main-Fight' be my next song, fairness' self!
Its subject—Contest for the Tragic Crown.
Ay, you shall hear none else but Aischulos
Lay down the law of Tragedy, and prove
'Best friend' a stray-away,—no praise denied
His manifold deservings, never fear—
Nor word more of the old fun! Death defends!
Sound admonition has its due effect.
Oh, you have uttered weighty words, believe!
Such as shall bear abundant fruit, next year,
In judgment, regular, legitimate.
Let Bacchos' self preside in person! Ay—
For there 's a buzz about those 'Bacchanals'
Rumor attributes to your great and dead
For final effort: just the prodigy
Great dead men leave, to lay survivors low!
—Until we make acquaintance with our fate
And find, fate's worst done, we, the same, survive
Perchance to honor more the patron-god,
Fitlier inaugurate a festal year.
Now that the cloud has broken, sky laughs blue,
Earth blossoms youthfully! Athenai breathes!
After a twenty-six years' wintry blank
Struck from her life,—war-madness, one long swoon,
She wakes up: Arginousai bids good cheer!
We have disposed of Kallikratidas;
Once more will Sparté sue for terms,—who knows?
Cede Dekeleia, as the rumor runs:
Terms which Athenai, of right mind again,
Accepts—she can no other! Peace declared,
Have my long labors borne their fruit or no?
Grinned coarse buffoonery so oft in vain?
Enough—it simply saved you. Saved ones, praise
Theoria's beauty and Opora's breadth!
Nor, when Peace realizes promised bliss,
Forget the Bald Bard, Envy! but go burst
As the cup goes round, and the cates abound,
Collops of hare, with roast spinks rare!

Confess my pipings, dancings, posings served
A purpose: guttlings, guzzlings, had their use!
Say whether light Muse, Rosy-finger-tips,
Or, 'best friend's' Heavy-hand, Melpomené,
Touched lyre to purpose, played Amphion's part,
And built Athenai to the skies once more!
Farewell, brave couple! Next year, welcome me!"

No doubt, in what he said that night, sincere!
One story he referred to, false or fact,
Was not without adaptability.
They do say—Laïs the Corinthian once
Chancing to see Euripides (who paced
Composing in a garden, tablet-book
In left hand, with appended stulos prompt)—
"Answer me," she began, "O Poet,—this!
What didst intend by writing in thy play,
Go hang, thou filthy doer?" Struck on heap,
Euripides, at the audacious speech—
"Well now," quoth he, "thyself art just the one
I should imagine fit for deeds of filth!"
She laughingly retorted his own line
"What 's filth,—unless who does it, thinks it so?"

So might he doubtless think. "Farewell," said we.

And he was gone, lost in the morning-gray,
Rose-streaked and gold to eastward. Did we dream?
Could the poor twelve-hours hold this argument
We render durable from fugitive,
As duly at each sunset's droop of sail,
Delay of oar, submission to sea-might,
I still remember, you as duly dint
Remembrance, with the punctual rapid style,
Into—what calm cold page!

Thus soul escapes
From eloquence made captive: thus mere words
—Ah, would the lifeless body stay! But no:
Change upon change till,—who may recognize
What did soul service, in the dusty heap?
What energy of Aristophanes
Inflames the wreck Balaustion saves to show?
Ashes be evidence how fire—with smoke—
All night went lamping on! But morn must rise.
The poet—I shall say—burned up and, blank,
Smouldered this ash, now white and cold enough.

Nay, Euthukles! for best, though mine it be,
Comes yet! Write on, write ever, wrong no word!

Add, first,—he gone, if jollity went too,
Some of the graver mood, which mixed and marred,
Departed likewise. Sight of narrow scope
Has this meek consolation: neither ills
We dread, nor joys we dare anticipate,
Perform to promise. Each soul sows a seed—
Euripides and Aristophanes;
Seed bears crop, scarce within our little lives;
But germinates—perhaps enough to judge—
Next year?

Whereas, next year brought harvest-time!
For, next year came, and went not, but is now,
Still now, while you and I are bound for Rhodes
That 's all but reached!—and harvest has it brought,
Dire as the homicidal dragon-crop!
Sophokles had dismissal ere it dawned,
Happy as ever; though men mournfully
Plausive,—when only soul could triumph now,
And Iophon produced his father's play,—
Crowned the consummate song where Oidipous
Dared the descent 'mid earthquake-thundering,
And hardly Theseus' hands availed to guard
Eyes from the horror, as their grove disgorged
Its dread ones, while each daughter sank to ground.

Then Aristophanes, on heel of that,
Triumphant also, followed with his "Frogs:"
Produced at next Lenaia,—three months since,—
The promised Main-Fight, loyal, license-free!
As if the poet, primed with Thasian juice,
(Himself swore—wine that conquers every kind
For long abiding in the head) could fix
Thenceforward any object in its truth,
Through eyeballs bathed by mere Castalian dew,
Nor miss the borrowed medium,—vinous drop
That colors all to the right crimson pitch
When mirth grows mockery, censure takes the tinge
Of malice!

All was Aristophanes:
There blazed the glory, there shot black the shame!
Ay, Bacchos did stand forth, the Tragic God
In person! and when duly dragged through mire,—
Having lied, filched, played fool, proved coward, flung

The boys their dose of fit indecency,
And finally got trounced to heart's content,
At his own feast, in his own theatre
(—Oh, never fear! 'T was consecrated sport,
Exact tradition, warranted no whit
Offensive to instructed taste,—indeed,
Essential to Athenai's liberty,
Could the poor stranger understand!) why, then—
He was pronounced the rarely-qualified
To rate the work, adjust the claims to worth,
Of Aischulos (of whom, in other mood,
This same appreciative poet pleased
To say, "He 's all one stiff and gluey piece
Of back of swine's-neck!")—and of Chatterbox
Who, "twisting words like wool," usurped his seat
In Plouton's realm: "the arch-rogue, liar, scamp
That lives by snatching-up of altar-orts,"
—Who failed to recognize Euripides?

Then came a contest for supremacy—
Crammed full of genius, wit and fun and freak.
No spice of undue spite to spoil the dish
Of all sorts,—for the Mystics matched the Frogs
In poetry, no Seiren sang so sweet!—
Till, pressed into the service (how dispense
With Phaps-Elaphion and free foot-display?)
The Muse of dead Euripides danced frank,
Rattled her bits of tile, made all too plain
How baby-work like "Herakles" had birth!
Last, Bacchos—candidly disclaiming brains
Able to follow finer argument—
Confessed himself much moved by three main facts:
First,—if you stick a "Lost his flask of oil"
At pause of period, you perplex the sense,—
Were it the Elegy for Marathon!
Next, if you weigh two verses, "car"—the word,
Will outweigh "club"—the word, in each packed line!
And—last, worst fact of all! in rivalry
The younger poet dared to improvise
Laudation less distinct of—Triphales?
(Nay, that served when ourself abused the youth!)
Pheidippides—(nor that's appropriate now!)
Then,—Alkibiades, our city's hope,
Since times change and we Comics should change too!
These three main facts, well weighed, drew judgment down,
Conclusively assigned the wretch his fate—
"Fate due," admonished the sage Mystic choir,
"To sitting, prate-apace, with Sokrates,

Neglecting music and each tragic aid!"
—All wound-up by a wish "We soon may cease
From certain griefs, and warfare, worst of them!"
—Since, deaf to Comedy's persistent voice,
War still raged, still was like to rage. In vain
Had Sparté cried once more, "But grant us Peace,
We give you Dekeleia back!" Too shrewd
Was Kleophon to let escape, forsooth,
The enemy—at final gasp, besides!

So, Aristophanes obtained the prize,
And so Athenai felt she had a friend
Far better than her "best friend," lost last year;
And so, such fame had "Frogs" that, when came round
This present year, those Frogs croaked gay again
At the great Feast, Elaphebolion-month.
Only—there happened Aigispotamoi!

And, in the midst of the frog-merriment,
Plump o' the sudden, pounces stern King Stork
On the light-hearted people of the marsh!
Spartan Lusandros swooped precipitate,
Ended Athenai, rowed her sacred bay
With oars which brought a hundred triremes back
Captive!

And first word of the conqueror
Was "Down with those Long Walls, Peiraios' pride!
Destroy, yourselves, your bulwarks! Peace needs none!"
And "We obey" they shuddered in their dream.

But, at next quick imposure of decree—
"No longer democratic government!
Henceforth such oligarchy as ourselves
Please to appoint you!"—then the horror-stung
Dreamers awake; they started up a-stare
At the half-helot captain and his crew
—Spartans, "men used to let their hair grow long,
To fast, be dirty, and just—Sokratize"—
Whose word was "Trample on Themistokles!"

So, as the way is with much misery,
The heads swam, hands refused their office, hearts
Sunk as they stood in stupor. "Wreck the Walls?
Ruin Peiraios?—with our Pallas armed
For interference?—Herakles apprised,
And Theseus hasting? Lay the Long Walls low?"

Three days they stood, stared,—stonier than their walls.

Whereupon, sleep who might, Lusandros woke:
Saw the prostration of his enemy,
Utter and absolute beyond belief,
Past hope of hatred even. I surmise
He also probably saw fade in fume
Certain fears, bred of Bakis-prophecy,
Nor apprehended any more that gods
And heroes,—fire, must glow forth, guard the ground
Where prone, by sober day-dawn, corpse-like lay
Powerless Athenai, late predominant
Lady of Hellas,—Sparté's slave-prize now!
Where should a menace lurk in those slack limbs?
What was to move his circumspection? Why
Demolish just Peiraios?

"Stay!" bade he:
"Already promise-breakers? True to type,
Athenians! past, and present, and to come,—
The fickle and the false! No stone dislodged,
No implement applied, yet three days' grace
Expire! Forbearance is no longer-lived.
By breaking promise, terms of peace you break—
Too gently framed for falsehood, fickleness!
All must be reconsidered—yours the fault!"

Wherewith, he called a council of allies.
Pent-up resentment used its privilege,—
Outburst at ending: this the summed result.

"Because we would avenge no transient wrong
But an eternity of insolence,
Aggression,—folly, no disasters mend,
Pride, no reverses teach humility,—
Because too plainly were all punishment,
Such as comports with less obdurate crime,
Evadable by falsehood, fickleness—
Experience proves the true Athenian type,—
Therefore, 't is need we dig deep down into
The root of evil; lop nor bole nor branch.
Look up, look round and see, on every side,
What nurtured the rank tree to noisome fruit!
We who live hutted (so they laugh) not housed,
Build barns for temples, prize mud-monuments,
Nor show the sneering stranger aught but—men,—
Spartans take insult of Athenians just
Because they boast Akropolis to mount,

And Propulaia to make entry by,
Through a mad maze of marble arrogance
Such as you see—such as let none see more!
Abolish the detested luxury!
Leave not one stone upon another, raze
Athenai to the rock! Let hill and plain
Become a waste, a grassy pasture-ground
Where sheep may wander, grazing goats depend
From shapeless crags once columns! so at last
Shall peace inhabit there, and peace enough."

Whereon, a shout approved "Such peace bestow!"

Then did a Man of Phokis rise—O heart!
Rise—when no bolt of Zeus disparted sky,
No omen-bird from Pallas scared the crew,
Rise—when mere human argument could stem
No foam-fringe of the passion surging fierce,
Baffle no wrath-wave that o'er barrier broke—
Who was the Man of Phokis rose and flung
A flower i' the way of that fierce foot's advance,
Which—stop for?—nay, had stamped down sword's assault!
Could it be He stayed Sparté with the snatch—
"Daughter of Agamemnon, late my liege,
Elektra, palaced, once a visitant
To thy poor rustic dwelling, now I come?"

Ay, facing fury of revenge, and lust
Of hate, and malice moaning to appease
Hunger on prey presumptuous, prostrate now—
Full in the hideous faces—last resource,
You flung that choric flower, my Euthukles!

And see, as through some pinhole, should the wind
Wedgingly pierce but once, in with a rush
Hurries the whole wild weather, rends to rags
The weak sail stretched against the outside storm—
So did the power of that triumphant play
Pour in, and oversweep the assembled foe!
Triumphant play, wherein our poet first
Dared bring the grandeur of the Tragic Two
Down to the level of our common life,
Close to the beating of our common heart.
Elektra? 'T was Athenai, Sparté's ice
Thawed to, while that sad portraiture appealed—
Agamemnonian lady, lost by fault
Of her own kindred, cast from house and home,
Despoiled of all the brave inheritance,

Dowered humbly as befits a herdsman's mate,
Partaker of his cottage, clothed in rags,
Patient performer of the poorest chares,
Yet mindful, all the while, of glory past
When she walked darling of Mukenai, dear
Beyond Orestes to the King of Men!

So, because Greeks are Greeks, though Sparté's brood,
And hearts are hearts, though in Lusandros' breast,
And poetry is power, and Euthukles
Had faith therein to, full-face, fling the same—
Sudden, the ice-thaw! The assembled foe,
Heaving and swaying with strange friendliness,
Cried, "Reverence Elektra!"—cried, "Abstain
Like that chaste Herdsman, nor dare violate
The sanctity of such reverse! Let stand
Athenai!"

Mindful of that story's close,
Perchance, and how,—when he, the Herdsman chaste,
Needs apprehend no break of tranquil sleep,—
All in due time, a stranger, dark, disguised,
Knocks at the door: with searching glance, notes keen,
Knows quick, through mean attire and disrespect,
The ravaged princess! Ay, right on, the clutch
Of guiding retribution has in charge
The author of the outrage! While one hand,
Elektra's, pulls the door behind, made fast
On fate,—the other strains, prepared to push
The victim-queen, should she make frightened pause
Before that serpentining blood which steals
Out of the darkness where, a pace beyond,
Above the slain Aigisthos, bides his blow
Dreadful Orestes!

Klutaimnestra, wise
This time, forebore; Elektra held her own;
Saved was Athenai through Euripides,
Through Euthukles, through—more than ever—me,
Balaustion, me, who, Wild-pomegranate-flower,
Felt my fruit triumph, and fade proudly so!

But next day, as ungracious minds are wont,
The Spartan, late surprised into a grace,
Grew sudden sober at the enormity,
And grudged, by daybreak, midnight's easy gift;
Splenetically must repay its cost
By due increase of rigor, doglike snatch

At aught still left dog to concede like man.
Rough sea, at flow of tide, may lip, perchance,
Smoothly the land-line reached as for repose—
Lie indolent in all unquestioned sway;
But ebbing, when needs must, all thwart and loth,
Sea claws at sand relinquished strugglingly.
So, harsh Lusandros—pinioned to inflict
The lesser penalty alone—spoke harsh,
As minded to embitter scathe by scorn.

"Athenai's self be saved then, thank the Lyre!
If Tragedy withdraws her presence—quick,
If Comedy replace her,—what more just?
Let Comedy do service, frisk away,
Dance off stage these indomitable stones,
Long Walls, Peiraian bulwarks! Hew and heave,
Pick at, pound into dust each dear defence!
Not to the Kommos—eleleleleu
With breast bethumped, as Tragic lyre prefers,
But Comedy shall sound the flute, and crow
At kordax-end—the hearty slapping-dance!
Collect those flute-girls—trash who flattered ear
With whistlings, and fed eye with caper-cuts,
While we Lakonians supped black broth or crunched
Sea-urchin, conchs and all, unpricked—coarse brutes!
Command they lead off step, time steady stroke
To spade and pickaxe, till demolished lie
Athenai's pride in powder!"

Done that day—
That sixteenth famed day of Munuchion-month!
The day when Hellas fought at Salamis,
The very day Euripides was born,
Those flute-girls—Phaps-Elaphion at their head—
Did blow their best, did dance their worst, the while
Sparté pulled down the walls, wrecked wide the works,
Laid low each merest molehill of defence,
And so the Power, Athenai, passed away!

We would not see its passing! Ere I knew
The issue of their counsels,—crouching low
And shrouded by my peplos,—I conceived,
Despite the shut eyes, the stopped ears,—by count
Only of heart-beats, telling the slow time,—
Athenai's doom was signed and signified
In that assembly,—ay, but knew there watched
One who would dare and do, nor bate at all
The stranger's licensed duty,—speak the word

Allowed the Man from Phokis! Naught remained
But urge departure, flee the sights and sounds,
Hideous exultings, wailings worth contempt,
And pressed to other earth, new heaven, by sea
That somehow ever prompts to 'scape despair.

Help rose to heart's wish; at the harbor-side,
The old gray mariner did reverence
To who had saved his ship, still weather-tight
As when with prow gay-garlanded she praised
The hospitable port and pushed to sea.
"Convoy Balaustion back to Rhodes, for sake
Of her and her Euripides!" laughed he.

Rhodes,—shall it not be there, my Euthukles,
Till this brief trouble of a lifetime end,
That solitude—two make so populous!—
For food finds memories of the past suffice,
Maybe, anticipations,—hope so swells,—
Of some great future we, familiar once
With who so taught, should hail and entertain?
He lies now in the little valley, laughed
And moaned about by those mysterious streams,
Boiling and freezing, like the love and hate
Which helped or harmed him through his earthly course.
They mix in Arethousa by his grave.
The warm spring, traveller, dip thine arms into,
Brighten thy brow with! Life detests black cold!

I sent the tablets, the psalterion, so
Rewarded Sicily; the tyrant there
Bestowed them worthily in Phoibos' shrine.
A gold-graved writing tells—"I also loved
The poet, Free Athenai cheaply prized—
King Dionusios,—Archelaos-like!"

And see if young Philemon,—sure one day
To do good service and be loved himself,—
If he too have not made a votive verse!
"Grant, in good sooth, our great dead, all the same,
Retain their sense, as certain wise men say,
I 'd hang myself—to see Euripides!"
Hands off, Philemon! nowise hang thyself,
But pen the prime plays, labor the right life,
And die at good old age as grand men use,—
Keeping thee, with that great thought, warm the while,—
That he does live, Philemon! Ay, most sure!
"He lives!" hark,—waves say, winds sing out the same,

And yonder dares the citied ridge of Rhodes
Its headlong plunge from sky to sea, disparts
North bay from south,—each guarded calm, that guest
May enter gladly, blow what wind there will,—
Boiled round with breakers, to no other cry!
All in one choros,—what the master-word
They take up?—hark! "There are no gods, no gods!
Glory to God—who saves Euripides!"

Robert Browning – A Short Biography

He is the equal of any Victorian Poet that could be mentioned. However, Browning continues to be in the shadow of Tennyson, Arnold, Hopkins, Morris and many others.

Robert Browning was born on May 7th, 1812 in Walworth in the parish of Camberwell, London. He was baptized on June 14th, 1812, at Lock's Fields Independent Chapel, York Street, Walworth.

Browning's early years were certainly very interesting. His mother was an excellent pianist and a very devout evangelical Christian. His father, who worked as a clerk at the Bank of England, was also an artist, scholar, antiquarian, and collector of books and pictures. Indeed, he amassed more than 6,000 volumes of rare books including works in Greek, Hebrew, Latin, French, Italian, and Spanish. For the young and curious Browning, it was a wonderful resource, added to which his father was a guiding force in his education.

Many accounts attest that Browning was already proficient at reading and writing by the age of five. He is said to have been a bright but anxious student and to have studied and learnt Latin, Greek, and French by the time he was fourteen. From fourteen to sixteen he was educated at home, tutored in music, drawing, dancing, and horsemanship. Certainly, language and the arts were two areas the young Browning both absorbed and pushed himself towards.

At the age of twelve he wrote a volume of Byronic verse he called Incondita, which his parents attempted to have published. The attempts were unsuccessful and, disappointed, Browning destroyed the work.

In 1825, a cousin gave Browning a collection of Percy Bysshe Shelley's poetry; Browning was so enamored with the poems that he asked for the rest of Shelley's works for his thirteenth birthday. In fact, Browning then went the extra mile, declaring himself to be both a vegetarian and an atheist in honour of his hero.

Intriguingly it seems that the rejection of his first volume didn't dim his appreciation of other poets, but it appears to have stopped him writing any poems between the ages of thirteen and twenty.

In 1828, Browning enrolled at the newly-opened University of London. He was uncomfortable with the experience and he soon left, anxious to read and absorb at his own pace.

His education which, overall is notably rambling and lacks a structure that many of his artistic contemporaries enjoyed, i.e. excellent public schooling and then a degree at Oxford or Cambridge, may present many of his critics with ammunition to criticize, but alternatively his hap-hazard education certainly contributed to many of the references that baffled both critics and his audience, but they tellingly show the breath and scale of what he could turn words too. What others would call obscure references were, to Browning, remarkably obvious.

Browning's early career was very promising. His long poem Pauline (of which only a fragment was ever finished and published) brought him to the attention of the Pre-Raphaelite master Dante Gabriel Rossetti and his difficult Paracelsus (published in 1835) was warmly admired by both Dickens and Wordsworth.

In the 1830s he met the actor William Macready and was encouraged to develop and turn his talents to the stage by writing verse drama. But these plays, including Strafford, which ran for five nights in 1837, and those contained within the Bells and Pomegranates series, were, for the most part, unsuccessful.

During this period Browning began to discover that his real talents lay in taking a single character and allowing that character to discover more about himself by revealing further personal aspects of himself in his speeches; the dramatic monologue. The techniques he developed through this—especially the use of diction, rhythm, and symbol—are regarded as his most important contribution to poetry. They would later influence such major poets of the 20th Century as Ezra Pound, T. S. Eliot, and Robert Frost.

By 1840, with the publication of Sordello, the tide turned somewhat. Many thought he was being deliberately obscure, opaque beyond measure and his poetry for the next decade or so was not eagerly acquired or talked about.

As Browning attempted to rehabilitate his career he began a relationship with Elizabeth Barrett in 1845. He had read her poems and, being totally charmed by their quality, was determined to meet her. The poetess was better known than the younger Browning but suffered from a debilitating illness and was also subject to the harsh behaviour of her over-bearing father. Nevertheless, the new couple were soon inseparable.

Her father, as he did with any of his children that married, disinherited her. Despite this she had some money from her own resources and sensing that the best outcome for both the relationship and her own health was to move abroad the couple did just that. After a private marriage at St Marylebone Parish Church, in September 1846, they journeyed to Europe to honeymoon in Paris.

Their new life now took them to Italy, first to Pisa and a little later to Florence. There they absorbed life and one another.

But in the short term the literary assault on Browning's work did not let up. He was now criticized by such patrician writers as Charles Kingsley for his abandonment of England for foreign lands. Browning could do little to answer these attacks except to compose with his pen and continue with his poetical journey.

The Browning's were well respected, and even famous. Elizabeth health began to improve, she grew stronger and in 1849, at the age of 43, between four miscarriages, she gave birth to a son, Robert Wiedeman Barrett Browning, whom they nicknamed "Penini" or "Pen",

Intriguingly despite his growing reputation and return to form as a poet he was more often than not known as 'Elizabeth Barrett's husband'.

Work flowed from his pen that was to ensure his reputation as one of England's leading poets. When his collection Men and Women was published in 1855 it contained some of his finest lines. It was dedicated to Elizabeth. Life had begun to smile handsome rewards upon the Brownings.

Victorian society was very much taken with all things spiritualist. It was not enough to have command of much of the globe through Empire, they wished to know and explore wherever they could. The spirit world beckoned their interest. Browning dissented from this view believing it was all a hoax and a fraud. Elizabeth, however, was inclined to believe and this caused several disagreements between the couple.

They attended a séance by Daniel Dunglas Home, in July 1855. (Home was a famous and clamored after Scottish physical medium with the reported ability to levitate and speak with the dead). It is said that during this séance a spirit face materialised. Home then claimed it was the face of Browning's son who had died in infancy. Browning seized the 'materialisation' which turned out to be Home's bare foot. Browning had never lost a son in infancy.

After the séance, Browning wrote an angry letter to The Times, in which he said: "the whole display of hands, spirit utterances etc., was a cheat and imposture."

The Browning's time in Italy were immensely rewarding years for both their personal and professional lives. Browning encouraged her to include Sonnets from the Portuguese in her published works, these beautiful poems are undoubtedly one of the highlights of English love poetry.

Elizabeth had become quite politicised during these years. Engrossed in Italian politics (which was continuing to slowly re-unify the country), she issued a small volume of political poems entitled Poems before Congress (1860) most of which were written to express her sympathy with the Italian cause after the earlier outbreak of The Second Italian Independence War in 1859. In England they caused uproar. Conservative magazines such as Blackwood's and the Saturday Review labelled her a fanatic. She dedicated the book to her husband.

But in 1861 tragedy struck.

The couple had spent the winter of 1860–61 in Rome when Elizabeth's health deteriorated again and they returned to Florence in early June. However, these turned out to be her final weeks. Only morphine would now still the pain. She died in Browning's arms on June 29th, 1861. Browning said that she died "smilingly, happily, and with a face like a girl's .... Her last word was .... "Beautiful".

Her burial took place in the nearby Protestant English Cemetery of Florence. The local people were deeply saddened, and shops closed their doors in grief and respect.

Browning and their son were obviously devastated. Unable to bear being in Florence without Elizabeth they soon returned to London to live at 19 Warwick Crescent, Maida Vale.

As he re-integrated himself back into the London literary scene he began to finally receive the proper praise, respect and reputation that his works deserved.

Browning went on to publish Dramatis Personæ (1864), and The Ring and the Book (1868–1869). The latter, based on an "old yellow book" which told of a seventeenth-century Italian murder trial, received wide and generous critical acclaim. Although by now he was in the twilight of a long and prolific career, that had achieved some notable ups and downs, he was respected and indeed renowned for his talents and works.

In 1878, he revisited Italy for the first time since Elizabeth's death. He would return there on several further occasions but never to Florence.

Such was the esteem he was held in that The Browning Society was founded in 1881. Although he had never obtained a degree (something that set him apart from many other Victorian poets) he was now awarded honorary degrees from Oxford University in 1882 and then the University of Edinburgh in 1884.

In 1887, Browning produced the major work of his later years, Parleyings with Certain People of Importance in Their Day. Browning now spoke with his own voice as he engaged in a series of dialogues with long-forgotten figures of literary, artistic, and philosophic history. Unfortunately, both the critics and public were completely baffled by this.

On April 7th, 1889 Browning attended a dinner party at the home of his friend, the artist Rudolf Lehmann. The highlight of which was a recording made on a wax cylinder on an Edison cylinder phonograph. On the recording, which still exists, Browning recites part of How They Brought the Good News from Ghent to Aix, and can even be heard apologising when he forgets the words.

The recording was first played in 1890 on the anniversary of his death, at a gathering of his admirers, it was said to be the first time anyone's voice 'had been heard from beyond the grave'.

His last work Asolando: Fancies and Facts (1889), returned to his brief and concise lyric verse that was so popular. It was published on the day of his death on December 12th, 1889, Robert Browning was at his son's home Ca' Rezzonico in Venice.

He was buried in Poets' Corner in Westminster Abbey; his grave lies immediately adjacent to that of Alfred Tennyson.

Among the many who have publicly acknowledged their literary debt to him are Henry James, Oscar Wilde, George Bernard Shaw, G. K. Chesterton, Ezra Pound, Jorge Luis Borges, and Vladimir Nabokov.

Robert Browning - A Concise Bibliography

Here follows a list of the plays and poetry volumes published during his lifetime. Poems of particular worth are noted from within those volumes.

Pauline: A Fragment of a Confession (1833)
Paracelsus (1835)
Strafford (play) (1837)
Sordello (1840)

Bells and Pomegranates No. I: Pippa Passes (play) (1841)
> *The Year's at the Spring*

Bells and Pomegranates No. II: King Victor and King Charles (play) (1842)

Bells and Pomegranates No. III: Dramatic Lyrics (1842)
> *Porphyria's Lover*
> *Soliloquy of the Spanish Cloister*
> *My Last Duchess*
> *The Pied Piper of Hamelin*
> *Count Gismond*
> *Johannes Agricola in Meditation*

Bells and Pomegranates No. IV: The Return of the Druses (play) (1843)

Bells and Pomegranates No. V: A Blot in the 'Scutcheon (play) (1843)

Bells and Pomegranates No. VI: Colombe's Birthday (play) (1844)

Bells and Pomegranates No. VII: Dramatic Romances and Lyrics (1845)
> *The Laboratory*
> *How They Brought the Good News from Ghent to Aix*
> *The Bishop Orders His Tomb at Saint Praxed's Church*
> *The Lost Leader*
> *Home Thoughts from Abroad*
> *Meeting at Night*

Bells and Pomegranates No. VIII: Luria and A Soul's Tragedy (plays) (1846)

Christmas-Eve and Easter-Day (1850)

An Essay on Percy Bysshe Shelley (essay) (1852)

Two Poems (1854)

Men and Women (1855)
> *Love Among the Ruins*
> *A Toccata of Galuppi's*
> *Childe Roland to the Dark Tower Came*
> *Fra Lippo Lippi*
> *Andrea Del Sarto*
> *The Patriot*
> *The Last Ride Together*
> *Memorabilia*
> *Cleon*
> *How It Strikes a Contemporary*
> *The Statue and the Bust*
> *A Grammarian's Funeral*
> *An Epistle Containing the Strange Medical Experience of Karshish, the Arab Physician*
> *Bishop Blougram's Apology*
> *Master Hugues of Saxe-Gotha*
> *By the Fire-side*

Dramatis Personae (1864)
> *Caliban upon Setebos*
> *Rabbi Ben Ezra*
> *Abt Vogler*
> *Mr. Sludge, "The Medium"*
> *Prospice*
> *A Death in the Desert*

The Ring and the Book (1868–69)
Balaustion's Adventure (1871)
Prince Hohenstiel-Schwangau, Saviour of Society (1871)
Fifine at the Fair (1872)
Red Cotton Night-Cap Country, or, Turf and Towers (1873)
Aristophanes' Apology (1875)
   Thamuris Marching
The Inn Album (1875)
Pacchiarotto, and How He Worked in Distemper (1876)
   Numpholeptos
The Agamemnon of Aeschylus (1877)
La Saisiaz and The Two Poets of Croisic (1878)
Dramatic Idylls (1879)
Dramatic Idylls: Second Series (1880)
   Pan and Luna
Jocoseria (1883)
Ferishtah's Fancies (1884)
Parleyings with Certain People of Importance in Their Day (1887)
Asolando (1889)
   Prologue
   Summum Bonum
   Bad Dreams III
   Flute-Music, with an Accompaniment
   Epilogue

www.ingramcontent.com/pod-product-compliance
Lightning Source LLC
Chambersburg PA
CBHW060301050426
42448CB00009B/1715